MOUNTAIN
HOUSES

MOUNTAIN HOUSES

Photographs by Philippe Saharoff

Text by Gwenaëlle Leprat

Translated from the French by Liz Nash

STEWART, TABORI & CHANG, NEW YORK

Contents

The Key to the Chalet

It was very hot in that early summer of 1982, and we had been steadily climbing high into the mountains, right up to Rimplas, which is reached by a steep, winding road at an altitude of some 2,625 feet (800 meters). At that time this eagle's-nest village, high above the road at the bottom of the Tinée valley, which leads to the resorts of Isola 2000 and Auron and is sometimes congested with heavy traffic, did not yet have a hotel or a gourmet restaurant. We just needed to say hello to an old man in the village with whom some friends had struck up a friendship while passing through a few years earlier; this was a man who—we had been told—had sold his last cow, but still took an

interest in what was going on in the world, after many years of combining his position as a simple farmer with his duties as mayor. He immediately wanted to know more about these young city-dwellers who had appeared from nowhere, and offered us hospitality for a few days. Since we had no precise itinerary and were equally curious to know about him, we accepted. He rushed off into his house on the tiny village square, reemerged with an enormous old key, and walked ahead of us up the narrow cobbled street that climbed in a steep slope above the village. Coming in the opposite direction was water, flowing down an uncovered channel next to the terraced beds of the vegetable gardens on our right. On the left was a series of barns.

The old man stopped in front of the next-to-last barn, explained that the little street now turned into a path leading to the high-mountain pastures, and then turned the key in the lock. The large, rough wooden door opened onto a shadowy interior. He walked across it and pushed open the shutter on the one window, which had no glass in it; light poured into the large room, revealing a huge timber frame and a floor with uneven boards in which there were slits, indicating the existence of a lower level that could no doubt be entered at the bottom of the slope. Clearly handwritten on a sheet of paper pinned to the door were the words "Welcome to the barn of friendship." The room also contained a double bed, a table, two chairs, a bench, a pitcher, and some candles. He explained that water could be taken from the spring about 66 feet (20 meters) higher up, and disappeared to bring us some vegetables from the garden and some eggs from the henhouse. I can't remember what woke us up the next morning: the song of the water pouring down the little street, or the diagonal rays of light that filled the room, shining in through the open space between the top of the wall and the roof, and also through the cracks between the boards of the shutters. That morning cast a spell, the effect of which, combined with the freshness of the air, was permanent. In the days that followed, the old farmer, Armand, took us much higher up, right to the place where the spring was harnessed, and along the way pointed out his scattered barns, which were now empty and stood on steep slopes where these days the grass remained uncut. He was delighted when, from time to time, a shepherd asked to use these barns to shelter his ewes. The ones in the village and the chestnut grove were now quite sufficient to store the crops he harvested.

Less than a year later we returned with a plan to buy and renovate an old building. The stone houses in the southern Alps were very closely packed together, so we were more interested in a barn up on a hill. But there were none for sale; our friend Armand was more concerned with preserving his family's inheritance than improving his bank account, and there were no others on offer anywhere else for miles around. Our argument that they would gradually fall into ruin if they were not maintained had no impact at all.

What had been inherited from ancestors long ago must be left to the children, regardless of possible financial difficulties. On the other hand, we were always made welcome and treated with the greatest generosity, with bed and board given as a matter of course. Gradually we progressed from the status of strangers to that of friends, and one day we were given a room with its own separate entrance, just above the wine cellar, which also had a main entrance on the alleyway below. Since Armand was the last home distiller in the village, we were well situated spot to witness him distilling his eau-de-vie, but we still missed the poetry of the barn.

Back in the eighteenth century these mountain-dwellers, with their tough lives and sturdy characters, were the subject of a letter to Julie in *La Nouvelle Héloïse* by Jean-Jacques Rousseau—one of the first hikers to sing the praises of the mountains—written while he was crossing the Swiss Valais: "I would have spent all my time during the journey simply by being enchanted by the landscape, had I not discovered an even sweeter enchantment in the company of the inhabitants [...]. What can scarcely be imagined is their generous humanity, and the zealous hospitality they offer to all strangers who are led to them by chance or curiosity. I experienced this in a surprising way, I who was not known to anyone: [...] whenever I arrived in a hamlet in the evening, everyone came to offer me their houses with such eagerness that I had an embarrassment of choice; and the one I chose seemed so pleased that on the first occasion I mistook this ardor for greed. I was most astonished, however, when after I had made use of my host's home more or less as if it were a tavern, on the next day he refused my money and took offense at my offer, and it was the same everywhere I went. [...] Their generosity was so complete that throughout the journey I did not find anywhere to spend a brass farthing." This is the same world that John Berger, the English author who has been living for many years in a peaceful village in the Haute-Savoie, has captured wonderfully in a magnificent book produced in collaboration with the Swiss photographer Jean Mohr.

From the village of Rimplas, it took only a short trip over the Col de Colmiane, with the neighboring community's ski resort perched at the top, for us to arrive suddenly in the Vésubie valley, whose slopes are covered with mountain chalets as far as the Boréon Lake. The most beautiful of these, inspired by the architecture of the northern Alps, were built some time ago for the wealthy inhabitants of the Côte d'Azur. Other families followed their example, building more modest chalets as second homes, which enabled them to take advantage of both winter sports and fresh mountain air in summer. As a result, wood once more became a commonly used material in a landscape where, as everywhere else in the Alps, it had preceded stone before the Roman Empire. Despite the use of wood, found in abundance in the surrounding forests, which are gaining ground as the area's population decreases, the Savoyard appearance of these scattered chalets remains an oddity in comparison with the conventional architecture of the area.

Thus, each region of the Alps has its particular features, dictated by history and sometimes by chance. In Megève, where the rural chalet was the norm, architects were extremely surprised when Mme. de Rothschild asked them to build not a sumptuous house, as one would have expected, but a chalet: quite a luxurious one, of course, but the materials were stone and wood, in the local tradition. Her personal, spontaneous preference for what was in keeping with the landscape put this delightful, high-class resort on the map, and contributed to the craze for chalets.

Returning to Rousseau, at a time when high-mountain peaks still inspired terror in both local inhabitants and visitors, he wrote about how astonishing it was that, in the eighteenth century, mountains were not recommended as a physical and moral remedy: "It was there that in the purity of the air around me I truly began to unravel the real reason for the change in my mood, and the return to that inner peace which I had lost for such a long time. Indeed, it is a general impression [...] that on high mountains, where the air is pure and fine, one feels more ease in breathing, more lightness in the body, more serenity in the mind; pleasures are less ardent there, passions more moderate. Meditations take on an indefinable character of greatness and sublimity, proportionate to the objects which strike us, and a certain tranquil, exquisite pleasure [...]. It seems that in rising above the dwelling place of men, one leaves behind all base, earthly feelings, and that as one approaches the ethereal regions, the soul takes on something of their unchanging purity." He had no idea that in the future, the advent of paid vacations in both summer and winter would enable generations of city-dwellers to share in his enthusiasm.

As property has passed from one generation to another, the children of the Alps have gradually given up land and buildings in order to benefit from the rise in tourism in the mountains. Whether tiny or vast, authentic or brand new, what counts now is the shared dream of the "mountain chalet": a place where people can take refuge, as they did with those simple farmers in the past, and get away from it all to enjoy times of good cheer and intimacy with their family or a wider circle of friends. Old chalets are now being taken down to be rebuilt on a better base, or for their old wood to be reused. Since these materials with the patina of age are becoming increasingly rare in France, they are brought in from both Switzerland and Austria, where their quality is exceptionally high, and from Eastern Europe, where buildings are being dismantled in huge numbers. There are also techniques whereby new wood can be made to look old, much to the annoyance of purists. The traditional proportions of the exterior are still retained, but the windows, doors, and interior spaces have been reinvented in keeping with modern standards of comfort. Authenticity has become an outlook based on harmony between a landscape, a home inspired by traditional savoir-faire, and its occupants, rather than faithfulness to the past, which is eagerly presented to us by ecomuseums and a few enthusiasts.

In Rimplas, a son and grandson have taken over, along with Armand's widow, Isoline. While she prepares her incomparable gnocchi, or her *daube de sanglier* [casserole of wild boar] simmers gently on the stove, they ensure in their own way that the magic of the place will continue to surprise the passing visitor for a long time to come. Without disowning the past, they live the mountain life of today, the one that the natives who have stayed are learning to share with those who are coming back in retirement, others who have just come there to work, and people who are seeking the most restful place they can possibly find. ※

Stone and Wood

A Natural Living Environment

Depending on the region, the main material used in building homes is either wood or stone. In the northern Alps, Haute-Savoie, and the Beaufortin valley, chalets are made mainly of wood, as they are in the Aoste valley, the Valais, Bavaria, and Austria. In southern Savoy, as far as the Maritime Alps, mountain homes tend to be "chalet houses" built primarily from mineral materials, with chalky rubblestone walls, or the stone houses with tiled roofs that are seen all over the landscape. Even so, their upper floors are usually made of wood, which is an incomparable insulating material.

This distinction between the north and south of the Alpine arc is often used to explain the architecture of its villages, and in particular the variation in distance between their houses. Because wooden

houses were regularly destroyed by fire in the past, people learned to keep a distance between buildings in order to prevent fire from spreading, mainly, of course, to make sure that they wouldn't lose everything at the same time as their neighbor did. In addition, everyone kept stocks of wood to one side so that they could rebuild if necessary. Despite these precautions, fire often caused devastating damage, and there are far fewer very old wooden chalets left today than ones built in stone. They became much less vulnerable in the eighteenth century, however, when thatch on roofs, which had to slope steeply, was replaced by shingles (*ancelles*), otherwise known as *écrâves* or *bardeaux*; these long slabs of spruce were laid in several thicknesses and kept in place without nails by long wooden poles weighed down by stones. When they became worn, they only needed to be turned over to give thirty or forty more years of use, depending on their exposure. Elsewhere it was common for smaller slabs known as *tavaillons* to be nailed onto the laths of roofs, and also used as cladding on the fronts of houses. This did not, of course, prevent the slightest spark from setting fire to the hay stored in barns. In stone villages, there was less anxiety, and people could live close to their neighbors without feeling at risk. Another factor affecting regional traditions in architecture is the type of materials available locally owing to geological variations. In the upper Maurienne, for example, wood is rare, while scree stone is abundant. As a result, gables tend to be built in dry stone, sometimes covered in roughcast. The frame consists of enormous larch trunks, directly covered with *lauzes* (shale slabs), which form a gently sloping roof. In some cases, the authorities have tried to influence the use

of building materials, frequently expressing a distrust of wood and forbidding its use, in order both to protect the forests and to limit the disastrous effect of fires. Building methods also go back to the historic past; after the Romans moved into Savoy, bringing with them their more sophisticated architecture made mainly of stone, a strong Mediterranean influence could be seen in the southern Alps. In the eighteenth century, when stone took the place of wood in the Tarentaise and the Maurienne, villages became more closely packed and the number of houses increased, gradually spreading to the limits of the land available. The passages between these houses were often very narrow, and sometimes arched to extend onto the street, as in Bonneval-sur-Arc, the highest village in the Maurienne, which is at an altitude of 6,020 feet (1,835 meters). Clustered around its baroque church tower, this protected site still does not contain a single modern house, while at the same time it has become a resort where people come to ski, even in summer, on the glaciers.

The oldest wooden buildings are those that used piles of logs plugged with peat and often covered with a cob of clay and straw. This technique is being revived today by drilling grooves along the whole lengths of the logs, which enables them to be fitted together and ensures that they are watertight without having to be covered. Now fireproofed, they are aesthetically pleasing, and just as resistant to atmospheric changes as a normal wall, if not more so.

Later, the inhabitants of the Alps preferred to use piles of beams, sawn from uncut tree trunks in rectangular or square sections. The delicate part of this procedure was putting the angles together, and the simplest technique was to fit them into one another by cutting notches into them, as can often be seen on the visible extremities of a chalet's exterior. Depending on the region, the height of the stone bases on which the logs or beams were piled varied from 20 to 32 inches (50 to 80 centimeters); sometimes the logs went up as far as the second floor, or even to the fourth, as in some *fustes* (log houses) in the Queyras. The stones for the base came from quarries, scree, or riverbeds, depending on the valley.

Types of stone used were granite, such as Mont Blanc protogine, and sandstone, which was equally solid, but also limestone, gypsum, hard schists, and pebbles. Not including the frame, a gently sloping roof could also be primarily mineral by being covered with *lauzes*, which are heavy slabs of slate schist, or with thin strips of sandstone or limestone. These could remain in place without being nailed on thanks to their weight, as long as the smaller ones were at the top of the roof and the larger

ones were placed toward the bottom and allowed to protrude over the edge to protect the walls.

The fronts and gables of houses were often clad with *tavaillons,* which played a major role as insulating materials, without blocking the air circulation that was necessary to prevent humidity. The need for insulation also explained the presence of wood inside the house. The types most frequently used were oak, which was dense and thick and, when used for a frame or floorboards, could last for centuries, and also the very resistant chestnut, larch, which was rot-proof, and fir, which dried quickly and was easy to work with. Pine came later from northern Europe, as did red cedar from Canada, which is found as shingles on roofs in Switzerland and in some valleys in Savoy.

Moving along the Alpine arc, which has no respect for borders, it becomes clear that it is impossible to define the chalet, given the infinite variety in which it appears. It is in passing from one region into another that the transitions can be seen: from two- or three-story chalets in the far south of the Alps to houses made of stone columns and wood in the Tarentaise; from small, entirely wooden buildings of the Beaufortin region, the Aravis, and the Chamonix valley to the *mazots* of the Valais; from collective homes in the En-Haut valley to ski resorts, and so on.

A conservation organization such as Maisons Paysannes de France, which is an official body, is there to ensure that this heritage remains alive. Its advice is to start by spending time observing in order to bring a project to maturity, and to note how discreetly an old chalet fits into the landscape. Of course, it is the materials and techniques used that will enhance its charm, but also the account taken of space, the proportions of walls, doors, and windows, and the local use of the slope. This is an approach that can apply equally well to an extension.

Most departmental branches of the Conseil d'Architecture, d'Urbanisme et de l'Environnement (C.A.U.E.) offer helpful guidance by making available to the public documents on heritage that list regulations and useful advice. Some local architects with great respect for the sites they build on are able to work wonders by juggling tradition with the unbridled creativity of a high-budget clientele. Even in indoor swimming pools, which you will find in the pages that follow, along with much simpler features, today—as always—water, stone, and wood reign supreme. ✳

Les Vincendières

The Authentic High-mountain Pasture Chalet

{BESSANS, FRANCE}

In a remote spot three miles (five kilometers) above the village of Bessans, the Personnaz family's chalet dates back to 1895. To our great delight, the current family members have remained true to their determination to keep it unchanged as a place that offers a move to summer pastures, these days not for grazing livestock but for the family itself. They all love to get together there for the feast of Sainte-Marie-Madeleine, the patron saint of the hamlet, after whom the grandmother of the family is named.

With its *lauzes* (shale slabs) on the roof and stocks of wood, this is an authentic high-mountain pasture chalet, which has never changed hands.

Since great-grandfather Michel-Adrien left the area in the 1950s to become a taxi driver in Paris, the chalet has remained exactly as it was.

It is in no sense a museum, however; he and his descendants have only one idea in mind, which is to go back up there, rediscover the high-mountain pastures of the Avérole valley, and enjoy living in harmony in this setting that still sings of the season of haymaking and reunions. Today, there is still one farmer who moves to the hamlet every summer with his cows and sheep, so the tradition remains alive.

It is not surprising that the place has attracted cinema set designers, who appreciate its authenticity; true, goats and hens are no longer allowed to sleep under the box bed, as they were in the days when men and beasts needed to keep warm, but nevertheless, there is not a single contemporary item for the eye to light upon. One can imagine the lengthy consultations that must have been needed to agree to the one exception to the rule: the installation of a simple shower. The fact that it is kept hidden behind wooden panels speaks volumes about the family's shared and unflinching determination to preserve the place. Visitors will search in vain for a television or computer screen; all you need up here is fresh air.

PRECEDING PAGES

The objects displayed on the wall were found in the adjacent barn. In the cellar, the milking bench and churn are still ready for use.

FAR LEFT

The box bed and its wooden chest evoke a whole era that the children love to relive when they come here on vacation.

LEFT

Under the low ceiling, which is characteristic of the high-mountain chalet, time has done its work; despite appearances, the wood has never been sanded or varnished. The family always keeps the wood stove humming, as an irreplaceable source of heat.

21

Perched on the hillside, the chalet with its balcony and small windows has an air of great simplicity under its magnificent *lauzes* roof. The piles of wood sheltered under the roof are still burned in the stove, which is connected to the chimney flue. The nearby barn is used as a toolshed.

The interior space is divided between the main room, which was once both a stable and a living room, a smaller one, which used to be the larder, and the summer kitchen, which contains the dresser and the large cooking stove. All the rooms have low ceilings covered in wooden laths and with rough-hewn exposed beams. The wood paneling that can be seen everywhere, except in the stable, has never been sanded or varnished. The visible veins in the untreated wood are simply the result of washing and scrubbing—which happened frequently when cheese was being made—and of gentle wear over time.

It is hardly likely that great-grandfather hung his wooden skis and snowshoes on the wall in the entrance hall where they are today, but what all these objects have in common is that they were once used, and one day emerged from oblivion, after lying for a very long time in a corner of the barn. Others have barely moved for many years, such as the churn and the barrel in the cellar, with the little milking bench still sitting next to it. Not to mention the chest that, along with the table and closet, represented the most important part of the family's furniture.

LEFT

This bedroom, with its copper bed, offers an unusual sense of comfort under the protection of a crucifix, which is said to keep away the danger of storms.

RIGHT

An improvised bouquet and a lace border: how to work wonders with nothing at all.

In the living room, where the stove hums, a fragile sense of privacy is provided by a cloth partition, which has the great advantage that it does not prevent the heat from circulating. Simple settings for the meal are placed directly onto the untreated wooden table. Bread, wine, and cheese are still essential foods here, no doubt as symbolic as the oil lamp that once supplied its flickering light in the evenings. It takes only very small touches to give a note of freshness to this rustic décor: a few strips of lace on the shelves, or a bouquet of wild flowers picked along steep mountain paths.

A staircase leads to the great-grandparents' bedroom, where the minimalist decoration has nothing to do with an attempt at modern style. The low ceiling is typical of high-mountain pasture chalets, and has exposed beams. The closet is built into the wall and has beautiful waxed wooden doors. The walls have been roughly coated with lime. The crucifix above the iron bed is a reminder of the importance of religion in these lives spent laboring and grappling directly with nature. The fact that there is a chapel in the hamlet itself also shows how many people once came up here in the summer period, when it must have been a hive of activity. Today, as in all the surrounding area, the chalets are closed down at the end of summer, and the occupants go back down to Bessans. And this charming village, right at the heart of the old Maurienne, seems wildly busy by comparison, as if its famous carved wooden devils were saluting the return to a less peaceful world. ✳

Le Mazot des Tines

A Tiny Nest with a Magnificent View

{CHAMONIX, FRANCE}

Purchased in pieces and reassembled in a garden in Chamonix, where it provides accommodation for visiting friends, this *mazot* has a picture window through which there is a magnificent view of Mont Blanc. Although this particular arrangement has nothing to do with the danger of fire, it is not entirely unrelated to the idea of a safe refuge where the family could go, like the *mazots* that often used to be built next to chalets.

LEFT

This beautiful larch staircase takes you upstairs to bed at the foot of Mont Blanc.

RIGHT

In the old days a *mazot* was always in semidarkness, with nothing but a door opening to the outside; the Savoyards of the past would have been dumbfounded by this light and airy view onto nature.

At that time, the family was moving to South Africa, and they were keen to have a haven where they could take shelter if they needed to return suddenly.

In fact, their time abroad went by as planned, and they were able to move back into their main home and use the *mazot* to put up visiting friends. From the outside, an old staircase in sanded larch provided shelter for the wood store, and led directly to the upper floor. The original layout of three small 320-square-foot (30-square-meter) rooms has not been retained. Although the *mazot* is tiny, it now has a kitchen that opens onto the living room, and an upstairs bedroom with shower and washbasin. To avoid going outside to reach the bedroom, it is now accessible from inside. From the living room, it is easy to forget how small the chalet is and concentrate completely on the view of Mont Blanc.

"For the layout I took inspiration from the way a boat is organized, and added lots of shelf space to make up for the lack of surfaces," says the mistress of the house, reminiscing with pleasure on the way in which she designed the space and directed the building work. "In the 1990s, people were just beginning to use deadwood, which then became so fashionable in the world of decoration. That was the wood I chose for the paneling, with

ABOVE

Everything is there,
even the mini-bathroom
with the fittings encased
in paneling.

RIGHT

An inside staircase now
leads directly up to the
bedroom: a real luxury in
rainy or snowy weather.

its characteristic slightly gray, subtle stripes in the fiber. It was found in the mountains, not far from here." To
create a contrast, she chose larch, with its more reddish color, for the floor and small shelves. The top of the
bar separating the kitchen from the living and dining areas is a large slab of Mont Blanc granite cut from the
block.

Fabrics that a friend arranged to have printed in Zimbabwe live happily alongside Marnaz pottery, in the
same spirit of openness reflected in this contemporary *mazot* entirely devoted to friendship. The ability to offer
independence to friends while keeping them close by is a luxury of which those mountain-dwellers of past times
would never have dreamt; their *mazots* were full of provisions, and had more to do with the need to survive than
with the joy of cheerful company. ❈

Guelpa

("Pretty Girl")

Comfort in a Very Protected Setting

{ARGENTIÈRE, FRANCE}

Ideally located in the massif of Mont Blanc and at the peak of the Aiguilles-Rouges ("Red Needles"), a cleverly designed, very comfortable chalet has replaced an old *raquard,* the local name for a large *mazot*—less than 540 square feet (50 square meters), which the family had made do with for years. The topography and narrowness of the site were obstacles that had to be considered before it became possible, without outside help, to design a building with the surface area of a real little mountain chalet. By separating the day part of the building from the night part, Michel was able to create his first chalet. Since then, improvement projects have come in thick and fast.

This contemporary
family chalet, located
on a very narrow strip
of land, overlooks the
famous Chamonix valley.

For a decade, the family went to their *raquard* every weekend.

Their predecessors had moved it to Argentière and fixed it up so that they could go there in winter. The couple were very attached to the place, and one day they decided that they wanted an interior that was better suited to their needs and those of their children, who were growing up. They had to be clever in order not to lose the tranquility of the hamlet of Argentière, the highest resort in the valley of Chamonix, which is very beautiful but also the second-largest tourist attraction in France and therefore very crowded.

Michel, who is an engineer, got to work with his portfolio after considering what needed to be taken into account: the best possible vista, the narrowness of the site, which backed onto the path and the little railway station, and the admirable desire not to block the neighbors' view over the valley. He tried desperately, and nearly gave up, then finally found the solution in a flash of inspiration; all he needed to do was "fold" the chalet along its length by forming an angle of 120° in order to create the floor space he desired. First, they had to part with the old *raquard* that had done them such good service. It was taken down, sold, and by an odd coincidence

taken back to its valley of origin. Delighted to have hit on his idea for the new chalet, Michel designed the project, had it approved by an architect, and gave the job of building it to a carpenter in Sallanches.

The chalet's name, Guelpa, means "pretty girl," and was chosen in memory of a relative who was very dear to the whole family. Today, you would sell your soul for the panoramic view from the wooden terrace, which had to be slightly raised in order not to disappear under the snowdrifts in winter. It is at the point where the "day" part intersects with the "night" part that you enter the chalet and immediately walk into a warm, inviting living room with plenty of space under the roof timbers. An L-shaped bench seat and a sofa form a cozy living area to sit in together after skiing. During the day, this main room lets in an exceptional amount of sunlight. In the evening, more subtle lighting is provided by a series of side lamps placed at intervals on the shelf, which runs all along the room. The painting on the wall is a copy of an Yves Tanguy done by the mistress of the house, who loves painting in her leisure time. Its bright, vivid colors are repeated in the Andean rugs, and create a warm atmosphere.

ABOVE

This feels like a refuge;
the space under the
roof is well designed
and contains plenty of
beds on the floor where
visitors can sleep.

The stone was built above floor level, as an extension of the bar. Behind it is a study area with a window, which is completely hidden from view. Michel regrets not having chosen a fireplace made of the local stone, which is the very highly reputed granite of the Chamonix valley.

As he himself says, it was his first house; these days he would spend longer designing his chalet. As for the budget, they had to make do with it, even if it meant ending up with a result that he finds a little too classic. "There were things that we were spontaneously attracted to for the decoration and paneling, but we were forced to go for options that were less contemporary." There are choices, however, that the couple would not go back on for anything in the world, such as the kitchen opening onto the living room with just a bar to delimit the space and make a place to pour a drink: "It's really ideal for having all the pleasure of getting together on the weekend as if we were on holiday."

The other side of the chalet, the "night" part, is where the bedrooms are; the couple wanted these to be spacious rather than have a larger number of them. The large room on the upper level, with mattresses on the floor, still has to be fitted out, and in the meantime is used as a guest room for friends. Its frame has a clever and original feature that enables building regulations to be met without losing too much space: The slanting rafters on the roof are supported by two beams rather than the usual single one, which, had it been in the center, would not have allowed a ceiling height of more than six feet (two meters). This intelligent choice adds charm to the room by giving it a wide central passageway and a high, elegant frame. ✳

Doors and Windows

A Melody of Carved Wood

During the long winter months, people in the mountains used to work with the abundance of wood that was available to them, to make not just their work tools but also all the objects that were needed in the household. They were not shy about using their talents to personalize their woodwork and the few pieces of furniture they had around them. In addition to this collective practice, they were quite happy from time to time to give some jobs to craftsmen or artists who were passing through, as they often did on their way between France and Italy.

From Savoy to the Tirol, cheerfully colored balustrades known as *palines* are on open view, displaying the virtuosity of their fretsaw carvings and openwork motifs laden with symbols: the ring-shaped rouelle, the edelweiss, the fir tree, the heart, the Savoy knot, and so on. At that time, wooden balconies were not used for lunching outside or lying in the sun; surmounted by a cross, they were essentially intended for drying crops, fruits in particular. They were covered by a wide, gently sloping roof, which also acted as a shelter for skilfully stacked piles of wood.

The doors of rural houses are especially sturdy, and display their charmingly naive moldings and carved motifs alongside their heavy hinges. It should not be forgotten that despite this diversity of decoration, under the wooden lintel and stone facing, three doors layered one behind the other were sometimes needed to keep the cold in its place. Not so, however, in the hay barns next to small mountain chalets that have been converted in recent times; here, no one was much concerned about draft-proofing the doors.

Nowadays these architectural features, long neglected and thrown away without the slightest regret, are much sought after by specialist firms whose address books are well stocked with the details of private individuals, antique dealers, and interior decorators. Salvaged and renovated, doors can occasionally be returned to where they came from in a building that is being restored to its original form.

This option remains the exception, however. Most antique hunters take whatever opportunities arise, and think in terms of Alpine heritage rather than a specific locality. An old Val d'Arly front door with a diamond motif above it would appeal to them all, and would be just as appropriate in the Maurienne as in Bavaria. These items bear no relation to modern building methods, and sometimes require the help of other skilled craftsmen, such as those working with iron, who can custom-make hinges to support an old door. Where interior doors are concerned, it is unusual to find enough of the same type. In the case of old windows, their dimensions do not suit our modern way of life. Although large windows with metal latticework are still very much sought after, in general the need for light has now overridden the fight against cold. As a result, the old cross-shaped window with two or four panes will probably be used as a frame against a wall, while another larger one can create a very charming door between two rooms in a chalet. Some things do not change, however; soft wood can be stained, whereas a noble wood, such as larch, will always be waxed.

When working with old salvaged wood, some mountain carpenters are able to reconcile the demand for authenticity with the need for comfort and sensitivity to the environment. For example, in a living room with a view over the valley through a huge picture window with old wood uprights, a small-paned window at the far end can subtly distill the light.

All of this has given a great boost to the revival of regional skills that for a long time seemed doomed to disappear. ✳

Mein Augen ich gen Berg
aufricht, dann ich
von oben rab Hilff zu
gewarten hab .

RIGHT

The room's tone is set by
the local-stone fireplace,
a figurative painting by
Didier Jean Alain, and a
coffee table made from a
cheese-draining board.

Les Carrats

Carefree Living

{VAL D'ISÈRE, FRANCE}

Hidden away on the top floor of a large chalet divided into apartments with a
wonderful view of the Olympian summit of Bellevarde is the warm, inviting home
of a retired couple who live in Val d'Isère all year round. Amid a décor inspired
by local tradition are pieces of family furniture with a history all their own, and
a host of objects that reflect the couple's passions, such as the collection of canes,
special treasures, and other pieces they have brought back from their travels
or picked up in the resort's boutiques. The mistress of the house has no great
enthusiasm for domestic isolation, and enjoys day-to-day life in the huge living
room with adjoining kitchen.

Hanging over the fireplace is a 1950s-style painting of a skier by the Saint-Etienne artist Didier Jean Alain, acting as a reminder of the resort's success in tourism, which enabled the couple to make their living and now provides jobs for their children.

On the other side, in the dining area, is a painting by the figurative artist Communal, showing the village of Tignes before the dam was built. Past and present live side by side in this large family apartment, with no attempt at uniformity of style, since this is first and foremost a home for living in.

The chalet looks as if it has been lived in for a long time, but in fact it is a modern structure put up by the architect Christian Martin. Evidence that the design is recent can be seen in its large terraces, which have a breathtaking view of the summit of Bellevarde. The interior space was designed by Alain Perrier, known for his renovations of the old Val-d'Isère. The central beam is made of a single piece, and rises to 26 feet (8 meters) above the dining area. The wood of the frame has been left untreated and waxed directly. The walls are wood-paneled, with laths rising vertically from the floor to a height of three feet (one meter), then placed horizontally above that. The bookcase, bar, and imposing hood above the fireplace, with its local-stone jambs, are all typical of Val-d'Isère.

The cast-iron plaque showing mountain chamois was unearthed in the flea market in Lyons. The rooms have large windows and are well insulated against the cold. The floor is made of old oak floorboards, which are quite wide and irregular. Although the wood is old, it is still alive: "After a while it began to warp, no doubt because of the dry air. We had it sanded, and since then it hasn't moved."

Under the high ceiling in the living area around the fireplace, the bright, warm red of two sofas upholstered in velvet is picked up in the more discreet, subtle red of the braids on the curtains, which are mainly in an off-white piqué material. The table in the living area is shaped like an arrow, and is in fact a board for draining cheese that was bought as an antique and then mounted on legs. On one arm of the white sofa is a rug brought back from the Americas. Lighting is mainly provided by spotlights, but there are also small side lamps for times when the couple want to have a quiet read, accompanied no doubt by the sound of the cuckoo clock they picked up in a flea market, its sophisticated carvings providing a contrast with the plain wood of the frame against which it hangs.

LEFT

Family and friends know
that the door is always
open for an impromptu
visit.

FOLLOWING PAGES

With the open kitchen,
guests can be entertained
with a mixture of
gastronomy and cheerful
company. A few family
possessions have found
an unexpected place,
such as this mirror above
the bath.

The dining table sits under a Blanc d'Ivoire ceiling light, and offers another opportunity to enjoy good company. It was made to measure from old wood by a craftsman in Bozel. The straight-backed chairs all around it were bought from Guaide, the cabinetmaker in Montvalezan. To show off the rustic tabletop, the place settings are laid on simple woven brown cotton mats from Thailand. The crockery was chosen from the Seccotine store in Val-d'Isère. Next to the fireplace on the dining area side is a magnificent collection of canes, to which the couple is continually adding, and which is an endless source of ideas for gifts for friends and family. "I wanted this large room without a break between the living area, dining area, and kitchen, unlike our previous home," says the mistress of the house. "It's much more pleasant to live in!" Behind the bar, the professional coffee machine is always ready for use when family, friends, or children also living in Val-d'Isère pay a surprise visit. While the decoration is mainly classic, the chrome appliances in the kitchen add a modern touch, as do the high stools, which came from the Galerie Saint-Vincent in Lyons. On the other side of the bar, the open-plan kitchen has a lower ceiling than the rest of the room, with magnificent transversal beams and impressive roof timbers that give the area a touch of privacy. Just above the room is a mezzanine in the roof space containing the guest room, where the double bed has a boutis Provençal quilt.

In her own bathroom, with its Italian tiles, the mistress of the house has placed a large mirror and family armchair, which are close to her heart. The motto of this interior seems to be to enjoy making your wishes come true without sacrificing the objects you love to the all-powerful demands of style. ❋

La Tournette

The Mountaineer's Refuge

{CHAMONIX, FRANCE}

This chalet's fairy-tale appearance is a good match for the exploits of the man who lives here. Built in the middle of Chamonix by two brothers who loved winter sports, it was taken on by Maurice Herzog, one of the great legends of mountaineering, who conquered Annapurna in 1950. He fitted the chalet out with his girlfriend in order to have a peaceful haven at any time of year. Erected in 1925 on a base in the shape of a Maltese Cross, the building has an octagonal shape and pointed roof which result in an interior architecture full of nooks and crannies, with mementos of Nepal living side by side with the old furniture.

An octagonal chalet from
1925 is home to Maurice
Herzog's precious
mementos of Annapurna.

ABOVE

The mountaineer has
enough books and
mementos to fill even this
large room. Alongside
the eighteenth-century
furniture, some of it
bought from the Pasteur
family, are some pieces
from 1925.

RIGHT

The former president of
the French Alpine Club
collects not only medals,
but also paintings of
mountain scenes.

The chalet's warm, cozy interior exudes a sense of peace.

"It really has a soul," says Sissi Herzog. It started with the two Ravanel Baguette brothers, who were hoteliers and wanted a large summer house in the middle of Chamonix. Two floors with a loft may sound fairly classic, but much less so was their dream of placing it on an octagonal shape inspired by the Maltese Cross, with four branches and eight points. The result? The kitchen is vast, as are the bedrooms, each with its own bathroom, while the innumerable nooks and crannies create an atmosphere that encourages intimacy. Proud of their achievement, the two sport-loving brothers had figurines of themselves—each wearing a pair of skis—attached to the weathervane on the pointed roof, from which they still watch over the eternal snows.

When the Herzogs bought this chalet a few decades ago, they made all the changes that were necessary to live there at any time of year. The heating, which until then was provided by wood fires alone, was modernized. The original roof, made of enormous, crumbly slates resting on a very heavy frame, was replaced by a covering that was easier to maintain. The renovation gave an opportunity to opt for wallpapers and fitted carpets, which at that time were regarded as the epitome of comfort.

The 1920s are still very much in evidence, however, in the original washbasins and faucets, and also many objects and pieces of furniture. These coexist happily with other much older ones, which the Herzogs bought

LEFT

Behind a succession of
small-paned windows,
the snow swirls and
leaves a white covering
on the trees in the park,
right in the middle of
Chamonix.

55

RIGHT

The bedroom reveals the octagonal shape of this chalet, inspired by the Maltese Cross with its four branches representing justice, temperance, wisdom, and strength.

from the Pasteur family, notably some pieces from the eighteenth century. On the walls, a collection of mountain paintings reflects the great passion of the climber, who was also president of the French Alpine Club. There may be treasures hidden away in the attic, but the house itself is strewn with souvenirs of expeditions, with a clear preference for Nepal, which remains the couple's favorite destination.

When the famous mountaineer also became deputy mayor of Chamonix, he moved into the house permanently. At that time the chalet's privileged location next to the Parc du Casino, the only wooded area in Chamonix, had every advantage: a town-center location with facilities such as guaranteed snow clearing, and the gentle calm that gives such a sense of well-being.

The decoration owes nothing to professional designers; it has been built up over a fruitful lifetime of adventures and encounters. The shelves on the walls are primarily occupied by books, many of them dedicated to this pioneer, who is still much admired. The ice axes and other expedition souvenirs, and the medals and trophies, blend in quite naturally with the other objects in the house. There is no need here for popular tradition to represent the mountains, which are not so much a beautiful landscape as a reason for living.

Like the kitchen, the bedrooms are huge, with odd little corners (due to the octagonal construction) that often contain windows. Warm colors, floral motifs, and piqué bedspreads add warmth to these large spaces, where the furniture is arranged delicately without ever creating a static décor.

All it takes here is snow swirling outside the windows and a few candles to believe that you are in a fairy tale where all your dreams can come true. The magic of the place is an alchemy between intimacy and openness to the world that is entirely in keeping with the character of Chamonix, this little community of 10,000 inhabitants which has achieved incredible world fame. It is a unique town, dominated to the south by Mont Blanc and to the north by the Aiguilles-Rouges, but in no way isolated; just 9 miles (15 kilometers) away, you can go into Switzerland via the Col des Montets, or indeed to Italy via the Mont Blanc Tunnel. ☀

RIGHT

This vast chalet is sheltered by a gently sloping roof, which is typical of traditional architecture.

La Tourterelle

("The Turtledove")

The Nobility of the Frame

{MEGÈVE, FRANCE}

Perched in the hamlet of Mas and protected by deep ravines, this is a vast chalet that nevertheless blends into the landscape as Savoyard chalets do, rather than competing with its natural environment. The south-facing living room looks out on the Aiguilles Croches, while other viewpoints in the chalet overlook Rochebrune and the famous Mont d'Arbois. The chalet's gray color—requested by Scandinavian owners who were not accustomed to brown wood—is unusual in the Alps, but has since been used elsewhere in Megève and the surrounding area.

LEFT

From the balcony, steps
lead down to a terrace on
piles with direct access
to the garden and swim-
ming pool.

RIGHT

A vase and its Plexiglas
base seem to be subtle
references to the color
and transparency of the
water.

Picture windows extending right up to just beneath the roof in order to flood the chalet with light: these are characteristic of a design by architect Bernard Rosier.

He started this innovation in the 1960s, when the only method of providing light was to pitch the roof timbers more steeply. The technique used here has the advantage of respecting the proportions of Savoyard architecture, and has now become a classic. Needless to say, he applied it to exploit all the available space in this chalet, which, although it does not look like it, amounts to nearly 5,400 square feet (500 square meters). The roof is covered in carved wooden tiles, and has the gentle slope of traditional constructions. It extends on one side to shelter a huge terrace on piles that leads to the garden and swimming pool.

At garden level is a large bedroom with its own bathroom, while the living room is on the floor above. It consists of a single space, running across the chalet from the main façade on the south side over to the north side, and uses the whole height of the chalet, right up to the roof space. With its split-level design and sliding wooden partitions, which can be closed when desired to create privacy, this interior space exudes a sense of peace and quiet.

Dark wood has been avoided on the inside as well as the outside. The fir frame is very restraining, because the architect was anxious to retain the "very bare style of the traditional Megève chalet." As a result the purlins

ABOVE

The choice of white for
the walls reflects the
priority given to light in
this interior design.

RIGHT

The dimensions of
the beams follow the
Megèves tradition rather
than the fashion for
larger frames.

and rafters are of moderate size, which goes against a trend in local decoration that is more inspired by the architectural heritage of Aravis or Grand-Bornard (with purlins of 16 inches [40 centimeters] instead of 10 inches [25 centimeters]). For the doors and skirting boards, fir is once again the main material. Bernard Rosier thinks very highly of this light-colored wood, which is also the least expensive.

The floor has irregular boards that are 6 to 8 inches (15 to 20 centimeters) wide, with perpendicular joints. Beneath it run water pipes for underfloor heating, which provides a surface temperature that does not, of course, exceed room temperature. In the very high rooms, electric films have been concealed under the laths to give a small but appreciable amount of extra heat.

To set off the wood, the walls are plastered, and because the surfaces are so huge, they are painted plain white. The two fireplaces in the enormous living room are modest in size and design. With their unadorned, straight lines and mantelpieces coated in white as an extension of the walls, they are placed on either side of

the space, which is organized around them. One is in the dining area in the roof space and separates it from the kitchen, while the other, which is almost identical, gives the living room a note of warmth and prevents a feeling of being overwhelmed by the height of the roof. The white sofas, glass-topped coffee table, and contemporary chairs in the dining area all contribute to the sense of harmony created by balance and restraint. And the few pieces of rustic furniture that have found their way into this light, airy space add a note of understated cheerfulness, as do the touches of bright color in the long curtains, rug, table runner, and cushions.

From the living area, a huge dressing room leads to the vast master bedroom in the roof space, which has a more markedly "wood" atmosphere. Most of the bedrooms with en-suite bathrooms are decorated very simply. They have fitted carpets rather than floorboards, the ceilings on the ground floor are low, and one would not believe one was in a chalet in Megève were it not for a few hunting trophies here and there, and above all the magnificent view of the mountain. In summer one can go from the south-facing balcony sheltered by a very fine overhanging roof onto the terrace at mid-level and then down to the garden and swimming pool below.

LEFT AND ABOVE

The bedrooms and
terrace are perfect places
to take a rest, especially
with their panoramic
view of Mont d'Arbois.

Only larch has been used on the exterior. It is already fifteen years since it was stained to achieve this wonderfully resistant turtledove gray.

All around the swimming pool are red cedar boards, which make it possible to sunbathe without burning the soles of one's feet. The pool is not closed in cold weather, either; anyone wanting to bathe in it can use a clever lock arrangement that forms part of the chalet's extension. This makes it possible to slip into the water under shelter, then swim out of the chalet and have an incredible view of the peaks—without having to cope with the outside temperature, since the water is heated accordingly. Here again, this is a real luxury that is kept discreet and expresses the art of living Scandinavian-style. ☀

Carnozet

The Exuberance of the Collector

{CRANS-MONTANA, SWITZERLAND}

Right in the center of the high-class resort of Crans-Montana in Switzerland, this warm, inviting apartment divided between three floors has an atmosphere of refinement. Guy Thodoroff has designed it in order to live there, combining French-style comfort with typically Swiss characteristics, but without yielding to the temptation of folk art. His own creations, special treasures, and old furniture seem to have been side by side forever in a harmony that is all his own. Thanks to his very particular artistry, this decorator, antique dealer, and collector of objects and houses has made it possible to forget how new the building is.

The apartment block is built into the hillside, and offers the occupants two different entrances.

The one most used is at the back of the building, where halfway along there is a beautiful rib vault leading to a staircase hidden by an old door. On the front of the block, an elevator goes directly up to the second floor. Its door is padded with nailed red velvet, in contrast with the wood paneling on the landing, where a sculpted bear from the Black Forest (late nineteenth century) serves as a cane holder and hatstand. Close by is a rustic chest carved from a tree trunk, a reminder of harsher times when furniture was limited to what was strictly necessary.

Designed by Guy Thodoroff himself, the fireplace is decorated with a stag's head in Brienz wood. On either side on the floor, the bestiary is completed by a pair of lions that were carved in linden wood and brought from England. The andirons are French. Upright, needle-shaped rock crystals are lit up after dark to add a touch of mystery to the evenings.

In keeping with Swiss tradition, the sofa faces the fireplace; it is surrounded by symmetrically arranged armchairs, and has a table behind it. The originality of the low table in the middle of the room eclipses the features of all the other furniture; having acquired a wooden bear as an antique, Guy commissioned the Brienz school of sculpture to produce three similar bears, all in different postures. Once the plaster models were approved, the bears were carved out of large blocks of assembled pine.

Used as the legs of the table, which has a pine top with cut-off corners, they give the living room an

PRECEDING PAGES

An antique bear from
Brienz was the model
for three others that
were commissioned
from the town's school
of sculpture. The stag's
head above the fireplace
is not a trophy, but
another woodcarving.

A beautiful collection of
nineteenth-century plates
from Thoune (in the
canton of Bern), which
were once sold as souve-
nirs, show landscapes and
celebrated events such as
World's Fairs.

LEFT

A dining room in the
spirit of the Swiss *carnozet* bistrot, a little room
next to the cellar where
people traditionally got
together in the evenings,
but here with an added
note of refinement.

ABOVE

The kitchen has a mineral
feel with its "bottle-
bottom" windows,
varnished Provençal
tiles, and contemporary
Thoune tableware.

A baroque bedroom in
which every object tells
a story, around the large
four-poster bed with no
canopy.

impish note, and highlight a coarse-woven Portuguese rug. All of this tempers the austerity of the nineteenth-century German armchair and Cresson sofa upholstered with finely stitched tapestry.

The wood paneling with French-style columns gives ample space to display beloved objects, books, and wax seal plates. Much space is devoted to Thoune plates, which were long neglected but in the end became highly sought after by private collectors. These Swiss souvenir plates were first produced near Interlaken in the eighteenth century, and show abstract motifs as well as landscapes. The display of nineteenth-century models occupies part of a bookcase and frames an eighteenth-century inlaid Bernese chest of drawers. Behind the sofa, on the table with turned legs and a red velvet cover, is another collection of German, Scottish, Turkish, and Japanese hunting knives.

The dining room is designed in the Swiss tradition of the *carnozet,* which is usually located in the cellars of houses, and is a place where people get together in the evening to enjoy each other's company in a "chalet bistrot" atmosphere. To reinforce its intimate character, it has a wood ceiling, unlike the living room, where roughcast with gloss distemper has been chosen to compensate for the lack of ceiling height. Under the window is a bench seat with gleaming cushions covered with a combination of eighteenth-century silk, velvet, and old tapestries. Along with some chairs, this seat provides ample room around the table, and matches the octagonal shape of the table, which is inlaid with walnut. Behind the seat, on either side of the floral brocade curtains, the wooden shelves are used to display blue and green German pots and Dutch vases in carved wood.

The kitchen has beautiful old door panels on the cabinets, and a pine floor inlaid with walnut. In keeping with these noble materials are the stained-glass leaded windows of the *cul de bouteille* ("bottle-bottom") type, which can still be found in Germany and Alsace, and the baked clay Provençal tiles varnished in dark green. The sink under the window is enhanced by an old-style faucet in red and yellow copper. A final authentic touch is added by the eighteenth-century Grisons table with turned feet. The dark tableware with edelweiss and other flower motifs is from Thoune, but is of contemporary manufacture. Behind a candleholder that has been turned into a lamp, the corner shelves provide a safe place to display more collection pieces.

The bedroom is decorated with great refinement and centers around a huge, very wide four-poster bed, which is composed of two old sections and has a fox fur cover. It is also very high, and contains large drawers. All around it the objets d'art come to life, with a Spanish statue of a penitent and Romantic German engravings framed in green velvet hanging above white Thoune lamps on skirted tables.

The guest room is much more restrained, and exudes a feeling of simplicity epitomized by the little northern Italian chair in the corner. The colored glass windows filter a gentle light onto paintings of snow

scenes, including one from 1870 by Malebranche. The ceiling and floor are in wood, while the walls are covered in sisal.

The small curio room has a particular sense of mystery. The divan in the alcove is heaped with beautiful, soft cushions, one covered in embroidered velvet and damask, and another in striped cotton. Hanging on either side of the figure wearing a fur hat in the central painting are small, typically Swiss wooden sculptures, which invite visitors to hang their hats on hunting horns, mounted in silver. The bears on the little Black Forest pedestal table are actually part of the table, and conceal a smoker's case. These rather cozy features are tempered by the presence of eighteenth-century écorchés and anatomical drawings. Opposite an early eighteenth-century chest of drawers, which may be Maltese, is a Dutch inlaid bureau bookcase and a Swiss chair, which serve as reminders that this room is also used as a study. ❋

RIGHT

Renovated with eighteenth-century wood and a great deal of love, this high-mountain pasture chalet has accommodated the members of the Albertville Olympic Committee.

Là-haut sur la Montagne

("High up on the Mountain")

The Jewel Box of Albertville

{MEGÈVE, FRANCE}

On the edge of a forest, this large high-mountain chalet overlooking the very chic ski resort of Megève looks as if it dates from centuries ago. Today, however, the original building is nothing but a ghost. Its current owner is an American woman who is fascinated by mountain chalets, and has completely dismantled it and redesigned every single room with the eighteenth-century-style furnishings she loves to collect. It is a consuming passion, which means that no detail is neglected in her highly refined use of space and decoration.

LEFT

Under a lintel, one of the chalet's forty doors is decorated with studs and carved with large Savoyard diamonds. Fittings had to be forged for the original hinges, which date back to the eighteenth century. The locks and keys came from Austria, and the handles were made by a craftsman in Annemasse.

RIGHT

An open view for a polar bear with clean lines, created by the sculptor Pompon. To mark the passage from one space to another, the mistress of the house preferred to use differences in level rather than doors.

After traveling to the four corners of the earth, she turned her back on Paris and left everything behind to live in the mountains, trusting in the powerful experience she had of feeling better here than anywhere else.

As with all those who are not from this area, it was as she learned more about the valley that she grew attached to it. She is interested in what characterizes mountain architecture, and is gradually becoming a real heritage expert, always ready to mobilize antiques dealers, many of whom have become her friends, and to travel all over the Alpine arc as far as Bavaria, so as not to miss a single auction.

It should be said that Megève was the village that reinvented the chalet during the 1920s, enabling the young architect Jacques Henry Le Même to give full expression to his remarkable genius. He had only just finished his training in the studios of one of the greatest interior decorators in Paris, and had taken refuge in the mountains for health reasons, when he had the good fortune to receive his first commission from Baroness Noémie de Rothschild.

Much to the displeasure of local society, she dreamed up the idea of asking him for a Savoyard farmhouse. So he traveled the length and breadth of the region, compiled details of agricultural buildings, and finally

BELOW AND RIGHT

A guest room decorated in the Tyrolean style, and the master bedroom in the roof space, all of which is reserved for the owners and Sweetie, their little hunting dog.

This bathroom is all in pale wood and is made to seem huge by the use of mirrors, while the other one has a more mineral feel with its slate copings.

created a vast chalet with seven bedrooms, not to mention the staff quarters under the large roof in two sections. Bathrooms, furniture, mosaics: he designed everything down to the last detail. It was the beginning of winter sports, the great lady had many friends, and orders poured in; Megève was launched. In this invention of an Alpine architecture that was both modern and traditional, Le Même reinterpreted the elements of local heritage very freely. Until then, farm constructions were based strictly on the local model for a dwelling, which corresponded to the mountain way of life in each valley. When the word "chalet" first appeared in the eighteenth century, it specifically denoted a small house in high-mountain pastures, but from now on the new-style chalet would mean any building in the mountains that contained some elements of local architecture. Le Même had no qualms about drawing on elements of folk art from central Europe and Scandinavia, both of which also produce large amounts of wood.

The current owner here takes inspiration from this approach, without seeking to modernize in any sense other than by adapting the interior to suit her own comfort. Her predecessors had fitted the chalet out in a simple style after buying it from a local farmer. When she purchased it in her turn, she had already accumulated a large number of old materials and objects of every sort, just waiting to be used. Apart from the frames and paneling, which are original, she took everything else back to square one, seeking advice from equally passionate connoisseurs such as her friend Alexandre Lambelin, and from craftsmen who were happy to have the opportunity to use their skills to the fullest. Dozens of cubic meters of wood and other pieces accumulated in the

RIGHT

The magic of nighttime
in the mountains, when
the outside lamps and
brightly lit fir tree
herald the approach of
Christmas.

FOLLOWING PAGES

The warmth of a
festive table under the
openwork sign of the
Savoyard heart. Beneath
the low ceiling, chosen
for its Swiss-style cozi-
ness, the whole living
room centers around
a magnificent double-
hearth fireplace.

course of her many tours were taken out of their protective casing to take their rightful place in a vast jigsaw puzzle intended to live up to her dream. In three years, the chalet was completely remodeled, both outside and inside. She readily admits that the whole plan goes much further back, and that the chalet is in fact the result of ten years of research that enabled her to refine her knowledge.

Her inspiration comes from the past, but she has no desire to live in an ecomuseum; every choice has been made in pursuit of comfort. She had no hesitation, for instance, in opting for low ceilings, which are characteristic of Swiss chalets and create a warmer atmosphere. One of these is in arolla pine from an old building in Saint Moritz, and another came from the oldest house in Val-d'Isère. She does not believe in doors, which close rooms off too completely, and prefers to delimit spaces by differences in level. To give a very gentle, subtly diffused light, she chose glazed doors and windows with small panes rather than large picture windows. As for the magnificent old Austrian fir floor tiles on the upper floor, she insisted that they be laid according to the rule book by a specialized carpenter who came over from Austria. Such attention to detail may appear excessive, but she has applied it with the same fervor to every aspect of interior decoration. Some pieces have been taken down and put back up several times before finding their final place.

A casual observer walking past this admirably rustic chalet would never imagine that it has received so much attention. Although its numerous pieces of eighteenth-century wood have been unearthed from the far reaches of the Alps, the proportions of the chalet are those of the local area. The stone base coated in white-wash is surmounted by wooden casings and a frame, which are assembled in the traditional style. This wood, patinated by age and without the slightest trace of varnish, extends over the whole width of the façade. The main entrance on the side of the chalet has a superb old door, which is carved and studded. It opens onto a large entrance hall with an eighteenth-century Kachelofen wood stove. The mistress of the house likes to receive guests on the ground floor, but the floor above is reserved for the couple. It is more intimate, and based on the same principles of interior decoration. Every single piece of old wood on the walls, with their niches and shelves, speaks of the past. This inspired chalet tells a whole story about the history of the Alps, and reminds us of the extent to which a restoration is also a work of creation. ❄

The Ballenberg

A Wealth of Heritage

The Ballenberg is a magical place for those who love chalets and the mountain environment. The canton of Bern, where it is located, is known as the birthplace of the Oberland house, the famous *chali* that has come to symbolize the Swiss chalet throughout the world, with its huge, gently sloping roof covered with shingles weighed down by large stones. Most of all, however, the Ballenberg gives the opportunity to see the extraordinary diversity of mountain constructions all in one place, since it is now home to about a hundred rural houses typical of the different Swiss cantons. These are chalets that, despite their historical interest, were destined for demolition; instead, however, they were saved by being carefully dismantled and then rebuilt exactly as before in this vast open-air museum. The little drying shed, which already stood on the perimeter of the museum, has been preserved, and one of the first houses on the site comes from Brienz, which is close by. Around it are three other houses, which are typical of the Bernese Oberland, including one from Matten, which clearly dates back to the seventeenth century; this can be seen from the continuous fluted frieze under its windows, and the unusual form of its purlin bearers. Its characteristic purlin-and-rafter roof is covered with shingles. From the first floor, stone steps lead up into into a huge kitchen, which extends right up into the roof space. Kitchens of this type allowed the smoke to circulate freely, and often took up the whole rear

of a house. The hearth has a trammel for pothooks, and was also used to make the farm's cheese. Jutting out behind it is the opening to the oven, which rests on wooden struts. Above it hang poles blackened with soot, which were used for smoking meat. The back of the house contains a bright living room, another small room, and a lean-to with a canopy, which shelters the little pigpen and the indispensable wood store.

Visitors can explore every last nook and cranny of these houses, knowing that everything is fitted out with the furniture, utensils, tools, and other objects of the period. In addition to this, the setting is brought to life with demonstrations of skills from the past, ranging from basketwork, making boxes from wood shavings, and cheese-making, to the calcination of whitewash, woodcarving, working with white copper, treating linen, and so on.

The houses are surrounded by gardens, meadows, and fields, laid out as they were in the past, and planted with flowers, aromatic herbs, vegetables, and fruit trees that are typical of their region, as well as grasses, cereals, and other forgotten weeds. Visitors are taken around in a barouche, which is an excellent mode of transport for discovering not just the architecture, but also the stock of farm animals whose traditional breeds have been preserved. A remarkable hay barn is used as a venue for evening festivities. ✳

Mon Jaja

("My Red Wine")

A Canny Antique Hunter's Hideout

{VILLARS-SUR-OLLON, SWITZERLAND}

In its magnificent location overlooking the Rhône valley and the Dents du Midi, Miriam's chalet is both spacious and picturesque. It started out as an average 1970s construction, with a flat roof and a surface area split into apartments; Miriam then gutted it and transformed it until it lived up to her dream. She took the wood from three old Austrian chalets that had been taken down, put it back to work, and used it for the frame, fireplace, and floors. The rest was created on the basis of drawings, objects adapted to a new use, and antiques unearthed in the hunt for bargains, which for her is an endless source of pleasure.

A Swiss chalet renovated
in the old style, using
old wood brought from
Austria.

The chalet's pedigree was established by the use of high-quality materials.

The roof now has green varnished tiles from Austria, and the ground around the house is covered in *lauzes* with uneven surfaces. Since the original pale wood façade had to be kept, it was sanded down and stained to give a more traditional effect. Miriam then painted a smattering of stenciled fleurs-de-lis onto it. Not satisfied with the choice of balcony balustrades available, she undertook to design them herself, having already decided that on the upper floor there would be a semicircular bulge to accommodate a round stone table. She then commissioned a carpenter to make them in larch, as well as the superb interior spiral staircase with the same open-work motifs as on the balusters.

Just three minutes' walk from the chalet, a little cog train stops to pick up skiers on their way to the slopes. When they return, next to the snow shovel is a washbasin in which they can clean their shoes before going inside. There isn't a standard object in sight; even the mailbox with a little decorative hen on top has been custom-made by a craftsman.

The living room is located directly under the frame, which was entirely re-created in old wood at the time of the renovation in order to give the building a roof worthy of a real chalet. The open fireplace at the center

PRECEDING PAGES

The owner is an inveterate antiques hunter; she buys first, then finds a place for each object later. She designed the balustrade for the balcony, which, under the snow, looks as if it has been there forever.

LEFT

The open fireplace with a local-stone hearth adds extra life to a living room decorated with a great sense of humor.

ABOVE

A Swiss cuckoo clock and some old clogs—every antique find has a history that appeals to our imagination.

RIGHT

There is a lightness of touch about the open-work balustrade, like the one on the balcony, on this staircase leading to the upper floor.

of the room has a hearth composed of flat-laid local stone and a hood in old wood, which is supported by stainless steel tubes in each of the four corners. Miriam chose this as the place to hang the Ben original, which states ironically in white on a black background that "Switzerland exists," a little phrase that gives food for thought, even though in this place we are more inclined to dream of mountain peaks. To protect the floor from embers, there is a screen around the fire consisting of a very fine steel mesh on rails.

On the wall there are some paintings with the familiar signature "Bonjour." The old furniture was picked up in Switzerland, and also in Alsace and Austria, where the same style of heavy, elaborately carved pieces can be found. In the living area, sitting among the old leather easy chairs, is a table that is just a hay sled with a sheet of glass on top. The same clever idea is repeated on the balcony, where the table is a small hay cart, surrounded by four chairs made of birch logs.

The curtain rods above the windows are old banister rails, bought long ago at a time when Miriam had no

PRECEDING PAGES

A sample of the owner's tableware collection is on display in this kitchen, which was specially designed and fitted by an Italian carpenter. The atmosphere is very different in the vaulted cellar where, in keeping with Swiss tradition, everyone goes in the evening to enjoy cold meats and good wine.

idea what she would do with them. Hanging from them are linen curtains, lined with padding and silk, with a pretty motif of hand-embroidered roses.

Sitting on the long wooden table in the dining area is an English pig trough filled with walnuts. From the cuckoo clock to the collection of clogs and numerous treasures from the farms of yesteryear, all the objects here pay tribute to the pleasure of hunting for antiques. Although Miriam never knows where they will end up when she buys them, and may well put them away for a while, she never moves them again once they are in place. The only objects that come from elsewhere are her husband's hunting trophies.

In the hurly-burly of the renovation, during which plenty of wine was drunk—hence the chalet's name, Jaja ("red wine" or "vino")—the idea of a restroom for guests was forgotten. It was added at the last moment

The box bed has a
wonderful view of
the mountain peaks.

RIGHT

Wood gives a note of
warmth to every last
detail of the bathroom.

in a little cabin right in the living room. The washbowl carved into the old wood and the stag wood toilet-roll
holder show just how much extra care was taken with it.

The kitchen has a sloping roof and modern equipment, which has been skilfully concealed. It was specially
designed and created by an Italian craftsman, hence the choice of a sink under the window in Italian pink granite
cut from the block. The tiles on both the floor and the walls, however, were picked up on the Ile de Ré. Miriam
has a passion for old tableware, but also collects fired earth ceramic carafes and goblets from Sarreguemines.

The lower floor contains five bedrooms, one the master bedroom with a mezzanine and fireplace, and
the others used as guest rooms. They are very restrained, and all lined with old wood, as are the bathrooms.
In the box bed, the snow-white piqué bedspread creates a very restful impression. The son of the family has his
bedroom in the basement, on the front of the chalet and opening to the outside. The beautiful stone staircase
leading down to it is not used only by him, however; also down there is the *carnozet* where everyone comes in
the evenings, Swiss-fashion, to enjoy eating cheese. On the same level, a corridor lined with fox furs leads to
a splendid vaulted wine cellar that offers other delights; this is where everyone gets together to eat snacks and
taste delicious Swiss wines. ☀

Les Barriaz

Return to the High-mountain Pastures

To rediscover the way of life in her native Montana, Peggy has fitted out her high-mountain pasture chalet and chosen to live there all year round, even though it means going down to Megève on skis when there is a lot of snow. Located on some 54 acres (22 hectares) of pasture land, almost no distance from the well-known ski area on the 2000 slope, the chalet has been named "Les Barriaz"; it might as well be called "world's end."

On the edge of the
forest, there is a *mazot*
close to this reno-
vated world's-end chalet,
which is often isolated
when there is a heavy
snowfall.

When Peggy, an American, grew tired of living in Paris and discovered this place at the end of the 1970s, she found it, quite simply, "magical."

At that time, the mountain chamois had no fear when they came to graze around the building. To transform a summer pasture area into a permanent place to live, Peggy had the chalet dismantled, gave every room a number, then put in solid foundations. The frame was then rebuilt exactly as before, except for the larger windows. These were considered essential to bathe the interior with light, but they still had the small panes of former times.

With her friend, decorator François Catroux, Peggy salvaged old wood, which was used to structure the room in the vast open space under the roof frame. For a brighter room in which they could use as much wood as they wanted without worrying about overloading the décor, the walls were painted white. In addition to the shelves, the old wood can be seen mainly in the sideboards, which create a separation between the living room and the dining area, where two rustic tables placed side by side enable up to fourteen people to dine, sitting on benches.

An imposing miller's ladder leads up to the mezzanine and bedrooms. These are designed to have a much cozier feel, with old Austrian fabrics in all but one; the mistress of the house has a copy of an eighteenth-century silk, rewoven in less fragile cotton at the request of the decorator, for her bedspread, pillows, curtains, lampshades, and even the remarkable Bavarian bench seat at the end of the bed, supported by two brown bears.

PRECEDING PAGES

The warmth of antique bric-a-brac prevails in the living room, which catches the first rays of the morning sun. Peggy's passion has enabled her to build a fine collection of wooden spoons and high-mountain pasture bells with their leather straps.

LEFT

The miller's staircase is a major element of the décor in this living room, which exudes a sense of harmony.

ABOVE

In contrast with the restraint of the living room is Peggy's exuberant bedroom with its exclusive fabric based on an eighteenth-century silk.

RIGHT

Lying on the bookcase made of old wood, against the background of a white wall, is a cat lounging among the books.

These extremes of refinement are in no way incompatible with the need to ski down to Megève to buy groceries in 20 feet (6 meters) of snow, or to devote day after day to breeding the Tibetan mastiff, a threatened breed that has found a peaceful haven up here on the mountain.

A quarter of a century after it was discovered, the chalet is not as isolated as it used to be, owing to the growth of Megève and its ideal location at the foot of the ski area on the 2000 slope. Today this is a highly sought-after spot where it would no longer be possible to make such a dream come true. Nevertheless, the chalet remains quite exceptional. ☀

Les Trois Coeurs

("The Three Hearts")

Serenity on the Mountaintop

{MEGÈVE, FRANCE}

At the foot of the Megève slopes, on virgin land on the Mont d'Arbois, two chalets linked by an underground gallery have recently sprung up, one for the family and the other for guests. Pine and larch salvaged from all over the Alps give the chalets the peaceful air of a Megève farmhouse. The designers did, however, take the bold step of supporting the wooden floors on two levels of coated stone, which is one more than in the traditional chalet.

ABOVE

A wonderful brim-full
indoor swimming pool
is placed at garden level,
while the vast living
room at the top has a
fantastically high ceiling.

"I am personally very attached to the houses where I have lived, and to those in which I choose to live," says Dominique, who did not hesitate to sell his first chalet when he found this magnificent piece of land on the slopes.

"I really wanted a chalet that was pretty! In fact, we were able to build two, which communicate at basement level. The first is a large family chalet, and the second is intended as a place for friends to stay, but also gives us a reception room on the top floor." Architect Pierre Duclos and interior decorator Alain Perrier often work in tandem, and they collaborated on this fine Megève project with its gently sloping pitched roof, traditionally constructed frame, and wooden façade rising above a two-story stone base. The craftsmen of Megève also mobilized their skills to create this perfectly restful interior. "Everyone put a lot of love into creating not just a beautiful chalet, but a chalet that was exactly what we wanted, in other words one that has a soul," recalls Dominique.

The large windows stretch right up to the rooftop, since the part of the chalet where light is most important is up in the roof space. The living areas share the chimney but are at different levels and have different uses: One is a cheerful barroom for entertaining, while the other is a more intimate relaxation room for private dreaming.

Wood is dominant everywhere, from the exposed beams of the frame to the oak floor and old wood panels that entirely cover the large living room on the top floor. It is never oppressive, however, thanks to the spaciousness of the rooms, the choice of simple furniture, and the quality of the light. In addition to the large size of the windows, the room also benefits from a more subtle diffusion of light through their small panes, which

The mistress of the
house's passion for
antiques is inspired by a
love of mountain art. The
mezzanine has a baroque
atmosphere with little
stag wood armchairs,
which celebrate the
mysteries of nature.

RIGHT

The décor is determined
primarily by the frame,
which is constructed in
the traditional Megève
way using old salvaged
wood.

ABOVE

Despite its nostalgic
style, everything is
brand-new in this profes-
sionally equipped kitchen
on the top floor of the
chalet.

RIGHT

The charm of the
Burgundy stone sink
with its stylish faucet
is emphasized by its
ideal position under
the window.

More intimate living areas offer the chance to relax in front of a good fire, while the main living room is intended primarily for entertaining guests.

A special dining area for the children, where jigsawed wooden bench seats and a little Alpine chair have been placed under a skylight. In the dining room, the chairs with their red covers add panache to this area with its sloping roof and door onto the balcony.

were so typical of chalets in the past. Under the center light, despite the impressive ceiling height, the large, soft sofas upholstered in natural-colored fabric, which matches the curtains and lampshades, give a note of comfort and harmony. The more rustic elements—leather easy chairs worn by age, an old wicker basket, and a low wooden farmhouse table—blend in well with the wood paneling and old floor, rather than detracting from them. Under its sloping roof, the bar is a cheerful place to have a drink or entertain friends. On the mezzanine floor, the bookcase serves as a guardrail, and cleverly conceals a study area, which offers peace and quiet under the natural light from the skylight. The treasured objects on display and figurative paintings of mountain scenes are the result of a highly successful team effort by the owners and their decorator, who picked them up on their travels in the Alps, the South of France, Spain, and especially Belgium.

Up in the roof space, the wood-paneled kitchen is equipped to a virtually professional standard. This efficiency is eclipsed, however, by the charm of the sink, Burgundy stonework surfaces, stylized faucet, and freestanding kitchen furniture in old wood.

The children have their own dining area, specially designed and placed right under a skylight. In the typical chalet spirit, the benches have been fitted into the wood paneling, and cleverly used to hide the radiators. The adults have the good fortune to be able to eat their meals in peace and quiet, on a long contemporary table that was found in L'Isle-sur-la-Sorgue. The mistress of the house has teamed it with very simple chairs, which she has brightened up with red covers. When the weather is fine, the family is only too happy to get together again to eat on the terrace, which overlooks Megève and its valley.

Let us forget for a moment that there is an elevator, camouflaged by fake or deliberately rusted doors, which serves every level of the chalet; let us instead go up the staircase to the intermediate floor and look at the bedrooms, all decorated in a clean, uncluttered style. Contrary to appearances, imagination is everywhere: for example, in the chests of drawers used as bedside tables, or even more so in the fireplace in the master bedroom, whose hearth also opens on the bathroom side.

If we go down a few more steps, the stairwell gives a view straight down onto an amazing brim-full indoor swimming pool. The water is heated so that it can be used at any time, and is just at the level of the snow behind the huge picture window, which is skilfully positioned . . . and never steamed up. The serenity that the setting exudes is reinforced by the choice of natural stone tiling and the effect achieved by cracked, wax-varnished paint. In this thermal, out-of-time atmosphere, only the benches made of untreated driftwood recall the dominant material of the region. In the evening, gatherings in the basement are not for nibbling on snacks in the Swiss fashion, but for dancing till dawn—unless, of course, you have agreed to be out on the slopes first thing in the morning. ❄

LEFT

There is a restful atmosphere in this bedroom with its wood paneling, fireplace, and two chests of drawers with curved outlines, which serve as bedside tables.

ABOVE

With its tubs, open shower on the travertine floor, and bench seat to rest on, the bathroom is in harmony with the Zen spirit of the indoor swimming pool.

From the Mazot to the Communal Chalet

A Joyful Diversity

A *mazot* is a tiny chalet that is beautifully constructed and hugely appealing. It was once used by families for the vital purpose of protecting their wealth; hence the completely disproportionate size of its enormous, carved lock. The danger came not so much from thieves as from the main chalet with its store of hay, which was always liable to go up in flames because of methane gas, and because the chalet had a large open fire that was lit continuously in some cases. After a fire it was always necessary to rebuild, but at least the family's property had been kept safe from the disaster. Located at some distance from the main building, the *mazot* is sometimes made entirely of wood—logs or beams—and sometimes has a stone base. One feature that never changes is that, to protect it from rodents and moisture, it is placed on a large, flat layer of stone, supported by stone or wood piles. It may also be covered with *lauzes,* shingles, or thatch, and is sometimes extended upwards or lengthwise. The lintel of the door is often covered with inscriptions. Depending on local custom, it was used to keep everything that mattered, such as seeds, grain, smoked meats, best clothes, and jewelry. In the Bernese Oberland, some *mazots* were even used for storing cheese. All of these were treasures, which explains why it was so important to build this special storehouse close enough to keep an eye on. There are exceptions to this rule, however; in the Valais in Switzerland, where these storehouses are known as *raquards,* they are sometimes grouped together on the edge of the village. This unusual feature is also found in the picturesque hamlet of Montgellafrey in the lower Maurenne, where they are gathered around the little square next to the washhouse and communal oven.

Once the farm was handed down to the next generation, the *mazot* was sometimes turned into a home for the elderly parents, which meant that they could stay close by to help out, and come back to the main chalet for meals. After 1800, the same concern for immediate proximity was shown in Switzerland by building the parents a *stöckli,* which was a more comfortable little wooden house containing a kitchen, a bedroom, and a living room. In the Alps, however, most older people were content with a bedroom with a closet and chest, or even just with a bed behind a partition in the kitchen. Nowadays, *mazots* are on the move; they are easily transported and reassembled by lovers of miniature structures and wood as a place where they can stay or put up friends. Some go so far as to place them side by side and create openings between them, in order to have the space needed to live there permanently.

At the opposite extreme are the huge chalets, once shared by several families, which can be found in Emmental (Switzerland), Austria, and Haute-Savoie. The large fir planks assembled vertically to divide up the interior add greatly to the solidity of these buildings, whose large spaces and numerous windows can give us a good idea of how life was lived there. Despite the perfect symmetry of the façade, there are differences here and there in the balconies, ornaments, and colors, which are usually signs of communal living. In Switzerland, at the time when chalets did not yet have chimney flues, and smoke still circulated freely in the kitchen right up into the roof space, families could prepare their meals together and then return to their own separate quarters by the staircases and galleries that led off this central room. ✳

Les Mélèzes

("The Larches")

A Thermal Ambience

With its wooden frame assembled in the tradition of the upper Tarentaise, this generously proportioned chalet is one of the highest in Val-d'Isère. It was recently built into the hillside, in the middle of the rocks and larches, with direct access to the ski slopes. On the inside it is a warm, inviting house, snugly enveloped in wood; the strong mountain influence in its design is combined with great comfort, so that it can be used all year round. One would never guess the amazing luxuries that are concealed behind its façade: a cinema room, a hammam, a sauna, and an indoor swimming pool with a view straight down onto the village.

A chalet in the midst
of nature that seems to
come straight out of a
fairy tale.

These extraordinary
little stag wood arm-
chairs should not distract
attention from an interior
architecture that has
created a wide variety
of spaces, all under an
impressive frame.

While the chalet was being built, the rocks and larches on the site were preserved so that the chalet would really blend in with its natural environment.

Neverthless, behind its larch casing is a state-of-the-art concrete construction, built at the behest of the owners, who wanted to benefit from both the charm of the mountain habitat and the most modern of comforts. The challenge was taken up by Alain Perrier, the developer originally responsible for the renewal of the old village of Val-d'Isère, who used his know-how to install heated floor tiles and a highly perfected system of home automation.

The house was turned into a chalet by the traditional technique of stacking and filling used for *mazots,* the small buildings constructed separately from the main dwelling as a place to keep provisions safe from the risk of fire. The larch framework remains true to the local techniques of the upper Tarentaise, while the stone base comes from the Manchet valley in the surrounding area.

Those arriving on skis have direct access to the chalet through an elevator, the door of which is concealed behind several layers of rusty paint. There is also a large staircase leading to a vast living room consisting of a number of spaces, where the local-stone fireplace has a pyramidal hood stretching right up to the roof. With the large, intersecting transversal beams in the exposed wooden frame, and the mezzanine overlooking the living area from halfway up, the whole room is a symphony of larch.

It took some clever ideas and a large number of windows to let light in without giving up the traditional small panes in the glass. This was especially important since the walls are also covered in horizontal wood panels.

The same fascination with noble materials can be seen in the wooden floor, which was salvaged and laid by the traditional method, and has a surface area of no less than 5,375 square feet (500 square meters)! Tucked away in the mezzanine, from which hang a collection of Alpine bells, the office has also been constructed in old wood; likewise the bar, where the stools with seats covered in cowhide add a little touch of mountain refuge.

The living room, arranged around the fireplace, is very subdued with its gray sofas that blend with the curtains and take up the tonality of the stone. Behind the sofa, two stag wood armchairs lend a note of baroque refinement.

PRECEDING PAGES

Behind the chest, which was once an essential piece of mountain furniture, a Seccotine fresco is integrated into the high-mountain pasture décor. The kitchen has an unusually high ceiling, allowing space for a huge wooden range hood.

RIGHT

With its uncluttered décor, the bedroom has an atmosphere in which the exclusive choice of larch reigns supreme.

In this enormous room, a cheerful polychrome fresco of a cow surrounded by a wreath of flowers marks the transition to the dining area. Here, fourteen guests can sit together at a long family table surrounded by lovely little Austrian chairs. A sliding double door enables the kitchen to be closed off from the dining area.

The bedroom has a fragrance of cigars and caramel, and shows off the full richness of larch with its frame, horizontal panels, and two bookcases, one on each side of a fireplace that is also in wood and decorated with carvings. No objects have been added to interrupt this homage to wood, and everything blends together into a monochrome of browns: the large studded leather armchair, the bed linen and bedside lamps, and, of course, the traditional old chest and low tables on either side of the bed, which backs onto a large dressing room.

The magnificent bathroom, with its sloping roof, has a wonderfully relaxing atmosphere; the bath sits under a small-paned window, putting the bather's shoulders at the same level as the snow. Under a ceiling whitewashed in the style of a stable, the décor is once again in wood, with bathroom shelves recessed into the wood paneling and a fitted bathroom suite.

The children all have showers adjoining their bedrooms, one of which has a delightfully nostalgic feel with

A window above the bath
means that the mountains
are never out of sight.

its old gramophone and two bunk beds turned into box beds by a wood casing with jigsawed carvings. The palm trees on the Pierre Frey curtains, which also open on to small-paned windows, add a touch of exoticism that suggests sweet dreams of far-off horizons.

Who would guess that this old-style chalet has its own private cinema? In this case, the ever-present wood has to vie for star billing with the Paramount red of the velour on the large, made-to-measure seats and their footrests. In the absence of windows, light is provided by old projectors adapted to the purpose, until the magic moment when darkness announces that the film is about to begin.

A level of living space was sacrificed for the indoor swimming pool, where the mineral atmosphere breaks with the all-wood décor in the living areas. Under the exposed wood frame, the light from the large windows with net curtains makes the water shimmer and sparkle. The pool's surround is paved with *lauzes,* and the walls are covered in simple plaster. Only a wooden bench with a straw seat gives a reminder of the charm and warmth of the rest of the chalet. Nearby, a hammam and sauna designed in the same style offer further opportunities for relaxation. ✳

LEFT

The retro red tonalities
in the projection room
create a sense of the
Paramount style.

ABOVE

With its two enclosed
bunk beds, this child's
bedroom makes it easy
for a friend to stay for a
sleepover.

The view over Val-d'Isère is set off by the very mineral décor of the swimming pool, with its surround of *lauzes* from Luzern.

139

Cornaline

("Cornelian")

A Cloak of Old Wood

This vast chalet in Megève takes its name from cornelian, a brown mountain quartz specked with gold. Designed by the developer Patrick Sanyas on the basis of the forms and spaces of the farms in Savoy, the cornelian farm is a vacation home for a family from Rome who fell in love with the site. Three minutes' walk from the center of the resort, the chalet overlooks a charming stream and has an incomparable view of Mont Blanc from its large terraces. Sheltered at garden level behind huge picture windows, a swimming pool lined with pebbles offers the chance for a refreshing dip.

A gently sloping, two-sided roof, a balcony, and a chimney: all of these are typical of the Savoyard farmhouse. But the concrete structure is skilfully covered by an old wood frame.

RIGHT

An allusion to mountain streams: the swimming pool is lined entirely with pebbles.

We want a family chalet that's truly unique!

This was the imperious desire expressed by both the young developer, who was determined to create two similiar buildings, and his Italian clients. Having chosen the materials and decided on some fittings with Patrick Sanyas, the clients adopted his plans, which were finalized by the architectural firm of Bruno Perrin. From the outside, no one would ever guess that this Savoyard farmhouse, characterized by its gently sloping two-sided roof and balcony, rests on a brand-new concrete structure. At the same time, however, the frames, which are not load-bearing, are in old wood, as are all the facings, exterior casings, and interior panels. Over a habitable

surface of roughly 8,600 square feet (800 square meters), including terraces, the wood represents centuries of accumulated history. Skilfully assembled and combined, they also form the structure of the wide canopy on the outside of the chalet that shelters the entrance.

This old wood is more and more difficult to find in Haute-Savoie, and so has also been brought from the area around Lake Constance, between Switzerland and Austria, where the best pieces are now to be found.

The whole structure has been protected from insect infestations by an injection treatment. Where the floor is concerned, however, because the chalet has underfloor heating, it has been necessary to lay new wooden floorboards of lesser thickness, along with local-stone slabs in some of the rooms. The floorboards are in a traditional design, consisting of wide strips of irregular length, and are, of course, waxed.

From the large entrance hall, a flight of steps leads up to the living room, where a huge frame joins the top of the chalet's roof at a height of more than 16 feet (5 meters). With no need for concern about underfloor heating, the gallery above the living room is the only part of the house with an old wood floor. It contains a television area up in the roof space, and leads to an attic bedroom with a bathroom. The exposed frame, fireplace, and dining room furniture are all in a rustic style, but the copious space and light in the room enable the

mountain style to blend in elegantly with the luxurious comfort of a Chesterfield sofa and a stag wood lamp-shade. The windows in the roof and terrace add a discreet but essential touch of modernity to the dining area and vast living room.

The kitchen is a separate room. Equipped to professional standards for the preparation of gourmet Italian meals, the kitchen represents an activity that plays a vital role in the chalet's welcoming atmosphere.

The master bedroom and its large bathroom with a sitz bath are on the same level as the entrance, on the right-hand side. From here, it is only a few steps down to the chalet's most relaxing spot: a swimming pool heated to over 85°F (30°C) and entirely lined with pebbles. It is bordered by stone slabs and a wide wooden deck consisting of the same teak duckboards as those on the large outside corner terrace, which on sunny days

can be reached through the sliding picture windows. A hammam, a double changing room, and a bathroom add the final touches to this space devoted to well-being, which shares the garden level of the chalet with two more bedrooms and their respective bathrooms.

None of this prevents the master of the house from having a real basement with a fine wine cellar, and a service area under the swimming pool itself that houses its controls, including a dehumidifying system, and is big enough to walk around in and carry out all the routine checks. But is it just a matter of routine, when the charm of tradition makes luxury discreet and helps to provide limitless comfort? ❋

LEFT

The sitz bath contributes to the charm of a bathroom that is full of nostalgia.

ABOVE

The bed linens give a note of freshness that tempers the warmth of the surrounding wood.

Le Creux du Gypse

("Gypsum Hollow")

An Encounter with the Valley

As good Southerners, Véronique and Jean-Claude dreamed of a chalet that gave a feeling of living outside on the terrace. They bought one dating back to the 1980s but were disconcerted by the local tradition of attaching more importance to heat than to light, and they called in the architect Jean-Michel Villot. The frame with its local-stone base was preserved, but large picture windows were installed that brought a flood of light into this made-to-measure vacation home, where the family comes for a break in both summer and winter.

The renovated chalet,
with its added windows,
overlooks the Allues
valley.

Under the salvaged slate roof tiles, the brushed-wood balustrades on the façade conceal large windows that were installed when the chalet was renovated.

On the terrace there is an outside Jacuzzi, which the couple and their children take advantage of as soon as there is a ray of sun—an especially great pleasure, since the hotel business they run in Provence rarely offers them such moments of respite. Their preferences coincide with the original image of the resort when it came into being next to Courchevel in 1925: small chalets on large pieces of land with as few roads as possible, in order to conserve nature, and modernity that does not break with the original hamlet style of building.

The interior has been entirely remodeled, using a contemporary approach alongside the old wood style that is so characteristic of mountain dwellings. The owners wanted dark walls, which they consider more modern, so all the wood panels were stained after first being distressed to produce an aged effect. The fireplace surround, exposed beams, and shelves create a décor that is both gentle and warm, and fits in very well with the clean lines of the furniture. As in old houses, there is a cloakroom next to the entrance where skiers can leave their jackets and boots. The ground floor has a large living room with a dining area, which has a wonderful view over the Allues valley.

The chalet owes a lot of its charm to the use of contrasting materials: for instance, the wood paneling in the living room and its floor, which consists of large squares of tinted concrete laid between wooden crosspieces. Elsewhere there are black Henau stone floor tiles, matte or shiny, depending on whether they have been fired

PRECEDING PAGES

The horizontal wood panels have been aged, then stained. The clean, modern lines of the interior architecture are echoed in the electronic equipment in the living room and bedrooms. Coats and snow boots are left in the cloakroom at the entrance, just like in the good old days.

RIGHT

A warm invitation to lunch looking out over the mountain; the light makes the materials vibrate in a beautiful vanilla-chocolate range of color.

or sanded, which give real character to rooms that are often merely functional. In the kitchen, which opens onto the living room, this material is used in conjunction with stainless steel to create a decidedly contemporary effect. In the bathroom, on the other hand, it is used entirely on its own, producing a Zen effect that is particularly well suited to such an intimate space.

Facing the fireplace, which is constructed entirely in wood right down to the base, comfortable armchairs in mineral shades create a restful atmosphere. Sheltered from the flames under the glass pane on the coffee table is a collection of cones from various trees: fir, spruce, cembra pine, maritime pine, and Alep pine. They seem like a fragile link between Provence, where the family lives, and the mountains, where they come to relax. Apart from a few rustic objects here and there—a ladder made of untreated wood, and an old toboggan—the emphasis in the decoration is on subtlety and comfort. The lighting is also discreet; center lights are replaced by carefully positioned spotlights and halogen lamps. The bookcase standing out against a white background conceals an elaborate stereo system, which is divided between the shelves and the closets with wire mesh doors.

LEFT

Between the open
kitchen and the living
room, a closet with wire
mesh doors serves as a
bar, covered with a slab
of black Henau stone.

RIGHT

The old-style faucet has
an irresistible charm.

The same design has been used for the closets, which separate the dining area from the kitchen, and can also be used as a bar or serving area.

Meals in the dining area are eaten right next to an enthralling view over the whole Méribel valley. In a palette of browns and beiges, the straight-backed leather chairs surround an oak table with an impressive top. When the weather permits, the small stools with driftwood legs and curly wool covers are taken out with their matching table onto the terrace just behind the heavy cotton curtains.

Upstairs, the keynotes are privacy and cocooning, and everyone keeps to their own space. The rooms all have the same old chestnut floor, however, which adds a lovely note of warmth. On one side is the parents' bedroom: a wonderfully harmonious, light space in the attic, with the added benefit of the amazing mineral bathroom. The textiles play on color; the flowered fabric on the armchair contrasts with the colorful stripes on the bedspread and flannel curtains. As in all the bedrooms there is high-tech equipment here, but it is kept discreet enough under its wooden casing not to look out of place with the rustic "bundle of sticks" lamp. On the other side, the three boys' bedroom aims at originality with its well of light at mezzanine level and its bunk beds. In the basement, an extra bedroom has been added to accommodate visiting friends. Its wooden bed with scalloped borders, inspired by the Savoyard box bed, gives it a great deal of charm. To avoid the chore of removing snow from the car in winter, a small extension to the chalet now houses a garage. ✳

LEFT

ABOVE

Upstairs, the salvaged
old chestnut wood
contributes to the
cheerful intimacy of
the bedrooms. The
children's bathroom is
also in wood, whereas
the parents' is entirely in
black Henau stone.

The boatlike atmosphere
in the boys' bedroom
contrasts with the very
gentle ambience created
by the guest room and its
lovely scalloped box bed.

159

Frescoes and Woodcarving

Artists of Talent

In the evenings and during the long winter months, men used to carve tools, cutlery, grain chests, and so on, decorating them with stylized motifs. The inhabitants of Albiez in the Maurienne even went so far as to carve bottle shapes out of green wood logs; the wood then dried and contracted around a dry wood base, thus ensuring that the bottle was perfectly waterproof. Some woodcarvers used to travel around between Christmas and Easter to teach shepherds, who, at that time of year, finally had some time off from their flocks.

This no doubt explains why the work of craftsmen and artists was given the recognition that it deserved. When people had money to spare, they were only too happy to give these men work. Those from Italy and elsewhere would stop off during their travels, which took in the great Alpine valleys. Others would gather together in a village where their know-how was recognized; one such village was Brienz, where in 1868 there were as many as 1,605 woodcarvers! The activity had been launched by the local chamber of commerce; inspired by the dynamic approach to woodcarving in the Black Forest as a winter occupation for its inhabitants, the chamber hired a German master to teach his art to the people of Brienz. Commercial firms then distributed the objects they created throughout Europe and took custom orders for carved furniture. In 1859, Brienz caused a sensation at the World Fair in London. Later, this craft industry was saved from decline by the creation of a very prestigious wood-carving school. One need only pay a visit to the old chalets to see that the famous Bernese bear still reigns supreme.

The same specialization can be found in the Queyras area at Saint-Véran, the highest inhabited

village in Europe. In this forest environment, where the raw material is available in abundance, it was the shepherds who communicated their passion to the villagers. In 1930, Abbé Guibert decided to make this skill into something that would enable people to continue living in the area by developing the production of carved furniture. Today this art lives on thanks to the prestige of "Vrai Queyras artisanal de tradition" ("Genuine Queyras traditional craftsmanship") label, which guarantees the origin of the furniture; it has to be made of local *cembra* pine by a local craftsman, at least a fifth of its surface must be carved with traditional motifs, the wood must be pegged, the drawers must have dovetail joints, and so on. The characteristic carved rosette has become the symbol of the Queyras brand. Another development of popular art in Saint-Véran was its sundials. The most famous of these, by Giovanni Francesco Zarbula, are surmounted by fantastical animal figures, multicolored flowers, or a rooster, which is the emblem of vigilance. Others are more simply decorated, but they invariably have a motto.

In Engadine—the area around Saint-Moritz in the canton of Grisons—the painted motifs are even more expansive, with the magic of multicolored trompe l'oeil often covering the whole façade of a house. Geometrical heraldic motifs, flowers, animals, and inscriptions are created here by the sgraffito technique, which involves scraping off a layer of whitewash from a gray roughcast base. Often a chalet's decorations tell everything about it; a good example is a house in Abdelboden in the canton of Bern, whose façade has inscriptions telling the year it was built and the names of the craftsmen, the owner, his wife, and the friends who helped out, and finally some biblical quotations, which place the house under the protection of God. ✳

Pierre de Torrent

("Mountain-stream Stone")

A Hymn to Materials

Starting with an ordinary 1980s building ideally located near the village of Megève and the ski slopes, a mountain chalet like no other has been created. Its traditional outline blends in perfectly with the landscape. Inside, the contemporary emphasis is the result of a skilful mixture of boldness and harmony, using sensuous materials and colors taken from the mountain environment that punctuate the space without ever overcrowding it.

Piles of logs under the
asymmetrical two-sided
roof are purely for
decoration.

Having grown tired of Courchevel, the family spent some time in Megève, where they could enjoy its well-conserved charm, and also initiate their youngest girl into the joys of skiing.

They had viewed an ugly chalet built in the 1980s, but immediately turned it down: too deeply sunken into the ground, too dark, too cramped. At that time, it was only a question of seasonal renting. Then the house was put up for sale by a professional, who suggested that it had the potential to be transformed, and in the end it became their dream to make their nest there. Danielle used to run a style agency and was accustomed to creating houses all on her own. She immediately got to work with her notebooks and camera, and put together images showing details of the architecture, materials, and colors, all of which would help her concoct the interior of her dreams.

First, the original chalet was completely dismantled so that nothing was left but its load-bearing walls. It was embedded into a slope in a way that looked cramped, so leveling work was carried out to "lift" it out of the ground and give it the more graceful appearance it has now.

The priority was to put in large windows that would let in light, including on the north-facing side. The

PRECEDING PAGES

Spruce lends itself to
the modernity of the
lines here.

RIGHT

Located under a window
and between two pillars
covered with mountain
stream stones, the iron
fireplace is the central
attraction in the living
room.

façades were given new frames made of old wood salvaged in eastern Europe. As is often the case today, the railings on the western and northern façades have stocks of logs behind them, purely for decorative purposes, since it is not possible to gain access to them. All that remains of the old chalet in the end is a balcony. On the inside, the removal of the partition walls has made it possible to reorganize the use of the surface area, notably by opening up one large room containing both the living and dining areas, and creating an enormous master bedroom, the entrance to which is protected by a hallway.

With their great fondness for contemporary style, the couple agreed not to follow the local trend, but at the same time to be strongly influenced by the mountain environment and its natural shades. The use of gray sets the tone for a very mineral type of decoration; some of the walls are built in dry stone using rocks from mountain streams, while the floor and bathrooms are in slate. The plastered walls are also gray, revealing the natural color of the mastic. In counterpoint to this is the brown of the furniture and also the knotless spruce laths on the walls and ceilings, placed horizontally and then brushed, sanded, and stained in a cigar-juice shade. As with the grays, Danielle has played with monochrome by choosing a light wood for the dining room chairs to contrast with the old oak tabletop in the center.

A quiet corner, facing the mountain: the orange throw blankets and gray flannel add warmth to the very mineral atmosphere.

RIGHT

The same attention to materials is found in the kitchen, where meals can be eaten at a large wooden table surrounded by low units in brushed stainless steel with Brazilian slate work surfaces.

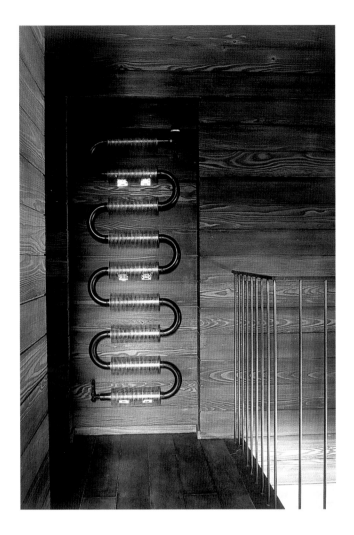

Based on the traces of an old structure that appeared when the chalet was being dismantled, a "transparent" metal-frame staircase came into being. It rises toward the mezzanine and divides the living room into two parts without blocking out any light. On the living area side, the mineral effect can be seen again in a very appealing tinted iron fireplace, which sits under a window. It was Danielle's wish that the fireplace not be placed on an opaque wall. The effect of this window is magical, because it means that at the end of the day, light comes into the room right to the very last ray of sun. The chimney flue is hidden in one of the side casings. Around the fireplace, the low part of the wall has compartments, which are used to store logs, books, and audio-visual equipment. Above these, aligned with the window over the fireplace, two other windows offer a unique view of the mountain. This bold option does mean that an extractor fan, with its gentle hum, is necessary to make the chimney draw.

All the furniture, or almost all of it, has been designed by the mistress of the house. From her sketches, the Alain Perrier Company created technical designs, which they then handed over to the craftsmen who made the furniture. Like the wooden top on the dining room table, the two rectangular tables in the living room have wrought-iron bases that are very light and come from the workshops of a wrought-iron craftsman in Annecy.

With its sofas covered in light gray flannel, the living room creates an overall effect of restrained line and color, enlivened by the warm tints of the Andean fabric casually thrown over the armrest. The same spirit is found in the orange throw blankets on gray flannel in the quiet area facing the picture window, and the very soft, reversible Shetland wool curtains. This is a very subtle finishing touch, and echoes the mountain-stream stone wall, in which studio windows form a large gap that separates the living room from the kitchen but does not isolate it.

The contemporary kitchen gives priority to low furniture in brushed stainless steel, creating a feeling of space. The choice for the work surfaces, on the other hand, was smooth Brazilian slate. Wood adds warmth to the room in a large, old table, which the family brought here from its previous holiday home. The porcelain double sink under the window also adds a rustic touch to the overall effect, which is all a matter of making choices that strike the right balance.

The stairs lead up to a landing and the bedrooms, including the master bedroom, which has the original balcony with its extraordinary view over the mountains. Instead of bedside tables, there is an overhead niche and two little lamps with wrought-iron bases. The adjoining bathroom is in slate, with gray plastered walls like those in the chalet's other bedrooms, which are always ready to accommodate broods of children and visiting friends. ✳

Le Grand Cerf

("The Great Stag")

The Contemporary Model

Blending in with the landscape and the hamlets in the surrounding area, this contemporary-style chalet remains true to the spirit that inspired the founders of the resort of Méribel back in 1925. The sport lovers in the family can just put on their skis and go straight out onto the slopes of the huge Three Valleys area, which is linked with Courchevel, Val-Thorens, and Les Menuires. The others then have all the time in the world to sit in the warmth and savor the view of the Allues valley through the picture windows of a Jacuzzi with a wooden deck that stretches right out to the snow.

The success of this restoration is due to the metal
sections and large panes
of glass, which open up
the chalet to light while
emphasizing the original
chimney at the center.

To make this large
window possible,
the weight of the
structure has been
redistributed onto
the sides of the
chalet.

The curve of the bar
contributes to the
skilful play of lines
in the interior archi-
tecture. The oak has
been whitewashed,
and then expertly
sanded to create an
uneven effect.

It's more of a winter chalet than a family home," says Michel. "It has a great location, and benefits our children, who come here regularly to ski with their own families."

Built of stone, glass, and wood, the chalet gives a great sense of lightness and transparency, a result achieved by retaining the structure of the existing building. It was already a ski resort chalet, rather than a high-mountain pasture cottage. One special feature was that it had no ridge purlin; this reflected the influence of Christian Durupt on the resort of Méribel, seen in the unusual unity of chalet frames there until the 1970s. Alain Perrier was the designer for the restoration of this chalet, and added large windows to its interplay of local-stone walls, wood frames, and slate roofs. To create such a window on the side of the chalet that is reached both by car and on skis, he removed some supports and redistributed the weight onto the sides. Against this open façade, the chimney rises in an elegant upward sweep along the original axis.

From the inside, the effect is equally spectacular; the living room is bathed in light coming in right up to the exposed wood frame, and faces both the fireplace and the snowy landscape. At night, the view of the forest next to the chalet is particularly magical.

The rooms have white walls, and all the oak fixtures have been whitewashed and then unevenly sanded to give a ceruse effect. A delightful touch of modernity is added by the use of embedded metal sections, notably in the doors. Long contemporary sofas in an L-shape face a coffee table made of the same sheet metal as the fireplace.

Under the mezzanine, the kitchen is within easy reach, and forms part of the living room. It is hidden by a beautifully curved bar whose shape lends a soft, cheerful touch to the clean lines of this interior. This is where the family likes to eat their meals with no fuss, just as if they were in a café. Light filters in through the small windows at the back, and the low ceiling creates a more intimate atmosphere, although it is still contemporary thanks to the dominant combination of steel and whitened wood. For those who like to take their time over their food, there is a dining room table close by, lit by a series of hanging lights in various shapes. In this large, well-conceived space, which is not overcrowded with furniture or objects, it does not take much to highlight a particular detail, such as the traditional bench in old brown wood or the brightly colored bunches of flowers, which stand out very agreeably against the harmony of whites and beiges.

The bedrooms open straight onto the terrace, and have all been designed in the same spirit, placing the

LEFT

The white walls and
embedded metal
sections in the wood
create a modern décor
very different from the
traditional wood-paneled
chalet interior.

ABOVE

The door of this
comfortable, unfussy
bedroom opens straight
onto nature.

emphasis on comfort and practicality. One notable feature is the high headboards made of wood panels. Some of these are placed vertically, while others are in staggered rows like a honeycomb. They are stained an oak color, and then bleached. The décor has been kept very simple so that the clearing up after a brief skiing trip is minimal, but the materials are of very high quality, in particular the fabrics used for the curtains.

Under the terrace is a large Jacuzzi for relaxing while enjoying a view straight out over the surrounding peaks. The large perpendicular window frames can slide open and give access to the wooden deck outside, which is right next to the snow. It doesn't take long to feel that one is away from it all while bathing in this perfectly harmonious place, where in addition to the sensuousness of the stone, wood, and water, the landscape is simply breathtaking. Everything here reflects a desire to conserve the environment without aping a bygone way of living. It is hard to imagine that it is built on the foundation of another chalet. ✳

Framed by a breathtaking view of the surrounding peaks, the warm water in this Jacuzzi seems to be coming from the snow.

RIGHT

A chalet composed of
curves and sweeping
lines, like the sails of
a boat setting out to
conquer the peaks.

Arketa

In Praise of Curves

{AVORIAZ, FRANCE}

At Avoriaz, a resort that was entirely created by Jacques Labro and other young
architects in the 1960s, Labro also built a chalet for himself. Breaking with
tradition, he designed it with great freedom of expression and a desire for
harmony, qualities that recently won him the highly prestigious designation of
"twentieth-century heritage." Here, everything celebrates the mountains, in the
same spirit that prevailed over the development of the famous car-free ski resort.
By sledge or on skis, life here is lived in a modern style inspired by the landscape
and tradition.

The softness of the sofas
and the charm of the
little concrete chairs
enliven the purity of the
décor.

The theme of the curve
is repeated in the half-
moon fireplace, which
evokes a bread oven from
times gone by.

Avoriaz is more fantastical than its festival…

Located on a plateau overlooking the valley, this 1960s resort linked to Morzine is both poetic and spectacular. Wood reigns supreme, with façades that proudly display their *tavaillons,* which are traditional tiles made of untreated wood. The architecture is also inspired by the contours of the terrain. The different levels are reached by interior passageways that fit into the natural slope like cultivated terraces. Roofs reaching all the way to the ground become confused with façades. The *tavaillons* age over the years, and depending on the type of wood used, their colors range from mink gray to *azelan* brown. Even inside the resort, snow is not cleared; the ski slopes intersect, and for transport there are sledges pulled by reindeer, or electric buggies. The inter-

play of loggias, cantilevers, rooftops, staircases, and unexpected proturberances presents the visitor with an architecture both poetic and astonishing. There are some more solid-looking buildings that sprang up at a later stage, but nevertheless the unity of style has been preserved.

It is not surprising that Jacques Labro, who was then a young architect and participated from the start in this conception of a new style of building in the mountains, should have built himself a home here as well. It was the dream location for complete freedom to design a new way of living attuned to this fantastical setting.

Blond wood and curved lines give a great sense of softness to open spaces bathed in light, and there is a huge picture window overlooking the Morzine valley. It is easy to imagine that one is in a boat anchored on the peaks. In this dream lookout post above the resort of Avoriaz, there is no need to worry about privacy, and therefore no need for curtains.

An intimate bedroom
and its accompanying
bathroom, both featuring
blond wood, are tucked
under the roof.

The interior contains generous spaces, punctuated by changes in level and gangways from deck to deck, as it were. This unusual feature is possible because everything rests on reinforced-concrete load-bearing walls and meshes of indented concrete. In other words, this chalet, which consists of three independent parts linked by a staircase, has no partition walls, in the classical sense of the term. For the architect, this was not just a technical and aesthetic challenge; he also wanted to create an atmosphere in which everyone would immediately feel at ease. The whiteness of the walls, with their huge, generously curved windows, contrasts with the blond wood used everywhere: for the beams, panels, floorboards, and so on. Every room communicates with another; the bedroom, with its wood-covered walls, opens onto a split-level living room, which in turn leads to the dining room.

Despite this, the space, with its minimalist decoration, does not feel in any way like a maze or a waiting hall; everything fits together harmoniously within this interior architecture consisting of downstrokes and upstrokes. The changes in level indicate the path from one room to another and play a part in the décor, as do the staircase and the Robinson Crusoe—style overhead gangway. For relaxation in the large living room, there are comfortable seats in warm colors, facing two little armchairs made of concrete.

Not a single piece of rustic furniture has found its way into this home, where the past goes back no further than the 1920s. Under the row of windows, parallel to the horizontal wood panels, a long wooden bench has been built into the frame and serves as simple seating for the table in the dining area.

Under the roof, at the far end of the gangway and feeling like the other side of the world, is a little bedroom, which also has an opening in the concrete, so as not to miss anything that is being said in the living room! There is another bedroom in the roof space, this one with a balcony. The basins and bath in the adjoining bathroom are built in, and as in the other rooms, a white wall maximizes the light provided by a small horizontal window. Intimately linked to the landscape, this interior expresses a state of mind that combines a sense of peace with openness to the world. ✳

The gangway that passes
overhead above the living
room opens onto a small
bedroom at the far end.

RIGHT

This former garage
has been skilfully
transformed into a daring
little contemporary
chalet.

Abate

The Love of Light

{VAL-D'ISÈRE, FRANCE}

This former garage in Val-d'Isère has been transformed into a chalet of glass and light, and now exudes a very contemporary joie de vivre. When Luc and Corinne bought the old garage, which was once a post office, they knew that they could only increase its surface area by 10 percent. Luc is a decorative designer by profession, and did not want to reproduce a traditional chalet; he decided instead to create something very different, a place that would have a sense of being "traversed by light."

The white walls and
graphic staircase with
no rail play a part in
the organization of this
space, which has been
thought through to the
last detail.

Sensuous materials: a
marble pathway leads
from the kitchen to the
wood stove, which is
playfully placed next to
the maple blinds and the
seat shaped like a root.

The existing building was taken down to insure that the foundations were solid, then the ground floor was rebuilt exactly as before, and two more stories were added above it. Resting on this delightful space are two columns cut from very dry tree trunks.

This is what has made it possible to create a light façade with the emphasis on windows. In fact the glass door is no more than 8 feet (2.4 meters) high, but the 24-inch (60-centimeter) strip above it is in turn surmounted by a 4.5-foot (1.4-meter) window. Facing this on the opposite wall is another glass door, which reinforces the luminosity of the interior.

"From the outside, it looks a bit like a little chapel or a doll's house," says Luc, "but the inside is bathed in light, which keeps us energized all the time and is a real joy." It is still possible to create a feeling of intimacy in the space, however, thanks to the blinds made of maple, and the 16-foot (5-meter) curtains that hang down from the roof space.

The original ridge of the roof from the garage was retained, but the two-section sheet-metal roof was replaced by traditional *lauzes*. Luc decided that between the stones there should be very discreet pointing composed of sand and white cement. For the inside walls, they made a bold choice: everything that is not glass is painted white.

The basement contains a garage, a guest room, and the laundry room. On the ground floor, in addition to the kitchen area and living room, there is a child's bedroom with a shower room cut out of marble.

ABOVE AND RIGHT

The contemporary style
contributes to the light
and airy feel of the décor,
which uses designer
furniture, some made
especially for this chalet.

The only concession to
Savoyard baroque is the
custom-made kitchen
furniture.

A magnificent pathway of marble leads from the kitchen to the wood stove, while everywhere else there are
wide maple floorboards, concealing an underfloor heating system. Like an overhead drawbridge above the living room, the mezzanine contains a small office and leads, across a corridor, to the master bedroom and its
bathroom with a floor-level shower.

With the exception of the kitchen, the spirit of the place is very contemporary. The decoration was handled
by Michel Boix-Vives, and owes a great deal to the designers, some of whom are very well-known, such as Augustin
Granet, who created the door handles and the dining-room table, which is one of only eight of its type.

Other notable pieces include the coffee table by Eric Schmitt, and the sofas and bureau by Martin Szekely.
The lamps were created by a sculptor in the Dordogne, while Michel Boix-Vives himself became involved in

ABOVE

An American patchwork
quilt and bedside tables
in the form of chests: a
world that dispenses with
nostalgia.

RIGHT

The sense of detail can
be seen even on the
beautiful wooden doors,
with handles created by
Augustin Granet, which
give a subtle suggestion
of stag wood.

producing the rug, which was made to order on the Rue Saint-Pères in Paris and was based on one of his collages. Finally, a few pieces of furniture were commissioned from Michel Contoz, the Savinaz carpenter.

In 1994, this chalet represented an original alternative to the traditional chalet. "Today, I would make some different choices," says Luc. "On the outside, for example, I would use lime instead of cement between the stones. But the minimalist feel that is favored by people who care about light is gaining ground in the mountains. Our chalet remains contemporary; of course, you can put a date on the architecture and decoration, but the pleasure of living here as a family, which inspired its whole design, has not shown a single wrinkle!" ※

Summer Landscapes

A Supreme Environment

Man has fashioned the mountains as the mountains have fashioned him. The landscape tells us more about his way of life than any book could. Based in the village, the mountain-dweller was in fact a nomad

who changed his residence by moving higher up as he reaped and mowed, up to ten times during the summer. As a result, there were a number of chalets known as "montagnettes," which were used for both shelter and hay storage as the work progressed. Sometimes the slopes were very steep, and the bales were rolled straight onto the upper floor of the building. Once this vital reserve of feed for the animals during the long winter months had been brought in, the shepherd would take his flock up to the high-mountain pastures, where the lush, abundant grass produced delicious cheeses. Any extra help was always welcome; the whole family worked together, and neighbors helped each other out as well, not just to bring in the hay, but also by lending a hand whenever necessary to friends and relatives. In return, they also helped each other to build chalets, and when the building was completed they celebrated with a party. These connections explain why, high above the village that was the center of social life, we also find strings of montagnettes and high-mountain pasture chalets, some more widely scattered than others. It was the quality of the grass that determined the value of a mountain pasture, bearing in mind that for cows it needed to be tall, flowery, and rich in vegetal species, while for sheep it had to be short. After climbing up a steep rise which sometimes had a *draille* (a sort of mule track with stone walls on both sides), they reached the high-mountain pasture, which was between 5,900 and 7,500 feet (1,800 and 2,300 meters), and thus above the tree line and below the level of scree, glaciers, and everlasting snow. This area could be on a plateau or in a sheltered little valley, where it was also possible to grow patches of vegetables and grains, and maintain grass meadows for mowing.

The chalets were smaller and more basic than those in the village, but did need at least one part for living and another for the dairy. Springs were harnessed upstream, both to water the animals and to keep the dairy products cool; the water arrived via channels, which had to be repaired and maintained. Around the chalet there were sometimes extra buildings, and groups of chalets often had a beautiful little chapel. The buildings were always located away from avalanche corridors, but sometimes an unforeseen snowslide, or just melting snow, meant that after long months of absence it was necessary to do repairs and remove stones.

It was a tough life, ruled by seasons and climate. The nourishing mountains also inspired fear, and no one would have thought of climbing the north face of a peak just as a heroic act. Nevertheless, these mountain-dwellers were freer than anyone living on the plains. There were overlords here as well, of course, but they quickly lost interest in land as harsh as this, and were content just to receive their dues without taking control of everyday life. The villagers' lives were therefore organized by a kind of self-management that can be regarded as an early form of democracy. Even so, there was no shortage of conflict between this communal rule and the royal and prefectorial orders that were issued. These were often intended to protect the forest, which nowadays, having once been so laboriously cleared, is steadily being reestablished on the pastures. Walking along the paths, you can still hear the murmur of stories from a past that is close enough for some survivors to relish giving accounts of it. ✳

Winter Landscapes

A World Enveloped in Snow

Nowadays the whiteness of a landscape covered with a thick blanket of snow suggests the tranquility of winter or the exhilaration of skiing down a slope. It was a very different matter when winter shut the inhabitants into their village for months on end or, worse still, forced some members of the family to take to the road so that there would be fewer mouths to feed.

It was because of this that Savoy sent generations of young chimney-sweeps out onto the roads of France, where they were wrongly regarded as rogues and beggars. There were also peddlers, sharpeners, oyster sellers, housemaids, hackney cab (later taxi) drivers, and so on. All these fine people returned for the summer as soon as work was available.

The snow seemed to envelop the villages of the Alpine arc in a long sleep, but underneath it, they were humming with life; every chalet contained those family members who had stayed at home, with their livestock, stores of wood, and all the food that was necessary for both people and animals. This was the time of year when the direction the village faced in was all-important; it could be more or less favorable, but it was always toward the south, on the sunny side, and all the windows in the chalet faced that way as well. The less popular northern side was abandoned to deep forests. This is why, despite the high altitude, it often freezes less in the villages than in the valleys.

In the collective imagination, the snow-covered chalet conjures up a picture of the ideal Christmas. Although people think that the weight of snow on the roof will do it harm, in fact, as with plants, the snow insulates it from the cold. What the inhabitants fear more is piles of snow falling off the roof, because they can damage or block the entrance to the house. It is no coincidence that the ridge of the roof always corresponds to the axis of the slope. In the upper Maurienne, the chalet is often buried to avoid such problems, with a very gently sloping roof on which snow can accumulate without sliding off. It also has wide projecting edges, which not only protect the stocks of wood on the balconies, but also ensure that, if piles of snow do fall off, they are kept away from the immediate surroundings of the chalet.

In areas sheltered by the massifs of the central Alps, the snowfall and rainfall are less; Modane, for instance, has only half as much snow as Megève, even though both places are at the same high altitude.

The advent of ski resorts changed everything. Suddenly the snow, which had seemed barely tolerable, was much sought after. In 1922 there began to be talk of resorts, similar to those that already existed in Switzerland and Austria. Two years after the first Winter Olympics, alpine skiing was recognized as a sporting discipline at Chamonix. After that, it became necessary, in less than half a century, to meet entirely new criteria in order to provide crowds of visitors with pleasure, freedom of movement, safety, and comfort. In the 1950s, the regional council of Savoy decided to create an entirely new international ski resort, based around the Three Valleys area; this was Courchevel, which suddenly sprang up on the high-mountain pastures. Since then, other urban developments containing tens of thousands of homes have appeared to accommodate a new kind of nomad, at altitudes regarded as uninhabitable since the dawn of time. Some ancient customs have prevailed, such as building on the south-facing side, and avoiding avalanche corridors; others have been flouted, however. Men of conviction have supported new trends; this is the case in Megève and Méribel-les-Allues, where, without copying traditional architecture, they have undertaken to build in harmony with the landscape and the existing hamlets. In the 1960s, Christian Durupt stated that it was not necessary to build higher and higher: "By staying within the tree zone we have the advantage of creating resorts that are of equal value in both summer and winter." ❄

The White Lake (Le Lac Blanc), with a panoramic view of the Mont Blanc range.

ABOVE

Nothing on the outside gives away how incredibly rich the décor is inside the "Chesa," as its most loyal patrons call it.

RIGHT

A meeting place created by prewar Swiss artists, along with the best local craftsmen. The frescoes and decorations here are better protected than in a museum, since the hotel is still run by the founder's family.

The Chesa Grischuna Hotel

{KLOSTERS, SWITZERLAND}

Located in the canton of Grisons on the Austrian border, the Chesa Grischuna Hotel was opened in 1938 on the site of a former railway station. It was designed and constructed entirely by the Zurich architect Hermann Schneider, to whom the Guler family gave carte blanche. Every detail contributed to the overall result, from the furniture to the objects, right down to the smallest table napkin. Skilled craftsmen were brought in, and the frescoes and woodcarvings were created by well-known artists such as Alois Carigiet and Hans Schoelhorn; for a long time, this made the Chesa Grischuna an international meeting place for artists. Over time, modernizations have been made to provide greater comfort, and renovation was necessary after the building was ravaged by fire, but all these changes have respected the place's artistic character. The hotel was singled out by the International Council of Monuments and Sites (ICOMOS) for "conservation and care lavished on a total work of art," with the result that today it has the enviable designation of "historic hotel." ✳

The Gstaad Palace Hotel

{GSTAAD, SWITZERLAND}

Above the elegant village of Gstaad, in the canton of Bern, a palace rises up to defy the mountain. At its heart is the story of a director and his wife who, after the war, succeeded in saving his hotel from bankruptcy by gradually buying back shares from the shareholders, with the help of friends and some loyal patrons, who then gave it a degree of fame it had not achieved since it opened in 1913. The third generation of the Sherz family has put a great deal of work into running the palace and giving it a sense of welcome. One example of this is the penthouse suite, under the roof between the palace's towers, which was opened in 2000. Its many attractions include a 1,615-square-foot (150-square-meter) balcony with a Jacuzzi and a spectacular view. Its chalet-style décor has exposed beams, plain wood panels, very simple corner fireplaces, wooden window frames, and, in the Swiss tradition, Brienz bears, stag wood ceiling light shades, and frescoes. Nothing is ostentatious; the fresh fabrics, in a blend of floral and checked motifs, give the 2,600-square-foot (240-square-meter) apartment a note of slightly rural cheerfulness, which tempers the solemnity of the old furniture. From the sauna in the tower, you can look down over the village through large picture windows. After the success of this suite, two other slightly smaller ones have been created in the other towers. ✳

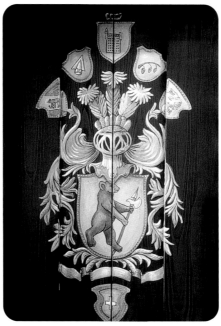

RIGHT, LEFT, AND
ABOVE

Mysterious from the
outside and warm on the
inside, this former palace
reserves its top floor for
suites.

The towers create unusu-
ally large interior spaces,
but the decoration is in
a refined chalet style,
from the wood frame
and Brienz bear to the
frescoes, colored wood
panels, and stag wood
ceiling light.

ABOVE

Built from salvaged old wood, this marvelous fir chalet dates back no further than 1998!

RIGHT

Charm and rustic simplicity do not mean lack of comfort; there is a feeling of mountain getaway here, but also of being at home.

The details are as carefully planned as the design of the spaces; for instance, the stairwell, with its amazing stone banister, is lit by a delightful window with a lace curtain.

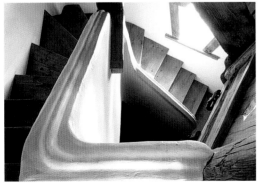

The Anchorage

{COURCHEVEL, FRANCE}

At the foot of the Bellecôte slope, which links the resort of Courchevel with the Three Valleys ski area, the Anchorage is a truly delightful chalet. The noble materials and simple, cheerful, traditionally Savoyard décor are so varied and graceful that one can easily imagine what a change of scene it is for those who spend a week there. The exterior, with its wood frame, sports blue shutters, a tiny "daylight" window, and a magnificent outside staircase with openwork fleurs-de-lis and carved wood decorations. Large windows, unobtrusive because they are under the roof, give the extra light missing in old chalets. The inside is a feast of wood, in the exposed frame, floorboards, mantelpiece, and horizontal laths on the walls. There is an abundance of charming detail: the wooden cornices decorated with scallops, the headboards with carved edges, the green and honey tiles in the kitchen, the various ginghams upstairs and in the kitchen, and so on. Because it is so pretty, the chalet feels cozy. Nevertheless, it has five bedrooms, each with its own bathroom, a steam room with a Russian bath, a Jacuzzi, and a massage room. A twin chalet, linked to this one in the basement, can also be rented, which means that friends can get together here in large numbers while remaining completely independent. ✳

The Mélézin Hotel

{COURCHEVEL, FRANCE}

Rebuilt from an old 1950s hotel, the Mélézin in Courchevel is now the only French establishment owned by the Aman Resorts group, which specializes in small, charming luxury hotels throughout the world. With regard to architecture and decoration, all the alterations were carried out by Edward Tuttle, a Paris designer, in the spirit of the grand residence favored by the hotel's director, Hélène Serane. On the outside, the balconies and casings are now a characteristic shade of taupe gray. An extra floor has been added, and the windows have been enlarged. The eighty rooms in the original hotel have been reduced to about thirty larger ones, three of which are suites. Dictated by the original building, the foyer has retained proportions that, along with the rooms on the ground floor—all in a row—help to give the hotel a sense of warmth and intimacy. Salvaged from a castle, the old oak beams and panels bring the whole setting to life in a very agreeable way. In addition, there are panels decorated with Indian frescoes, which have been waxed to give them the appearance of slightly patinated leather. The basement gives direct access to the slopes of the vast Three Valleys ski area, and was created to house a magnificent spa in Capri stone, with massage and beauty rooms, a swimming pool, and a gym. ✳

ABOVE, RIGHT,
AND LEFT

This old
Courchevel hotel
has been entirely
renovated, and
combines a limited
number of rooms
with an unobtrusive
luxury, placing
the emphasis on
privacy.

Thanks to the
hotel group's Asian
origins, the wood
fittings have been
given a very stylish
touch of exoticism.

L'Hôtel du Mont-Blanc

{MEGÈVE, FRANCE}

Right in the center of the village, this legendary hotel was extremely popular with artists in the postwar period, and still has a splendid fresco by Jean Cocteau. Recently, the Mont-Blanc has seen a return to its glory days, ever since it was taken over in 1994 by Jocelyne and Jean-Louis Sibuet, who have managed to combine an elegance worthy of the hotel's reputation with a touch of the same freshness and authenticity that characterize Les Fermes de Marie. Wall-to-wall carpets have been replaced by old wood floors, and drapes with pompoms have given way to superb Austrian textiles. There is also something magical about the way in which, for instance, finely carved English wood trim is placed daringly alongside a Savoyard dresser. There are about forty rooms, in which a sense of cheerfulness and charm is often created by small touches: for example, this canopy above the bed, made of light fabric and held back on each side by a tieback with a little skirted bedside table underneath. And when we look at the anonymous ancestors whose portraits hang along the wood panels, we are not so much awed as reassured. ☀

ABOVE

Today, wood reigns supreme again in the heart of Megève, and the Savoyard hearts on the balustrade are an invitation to rediscover the hotel.

RIGHT

Not a single false note: the freshness of the decoration brings a touch of lightness to more opulent furniture, which still fits in perfectly.

RIGHT

Famous throughout the world, the village of Les Fermes de Marie has relaunched the resort of Megève, combining luxury with rustic simplicity. Every bedroom is named after a flower, but edelweiss is at the top of the list of homemade spa products.

Les Fermes de Marie

{MEGÈVE, FRANCE}

Jean-Louis Sibuet is a native of Savoy, and has fulfilled a dream: to re-create a hamlet of times gone by in Megève, highlighting the value of traditional local architecture. His wife Jocelyne added the charm of a very rural style of decoration and a sense of cheerfulness, which make it a remarkably harmonious place. Classified as a four-star hotel, this extraordinary creation is a skilful blend of luxury and rustic simplicity. Since it opened, it has swarmed with visitors and given rise to the Compagnie des Hôtels de Montagne (Mountain Hotels Group), an organization made up of establishments with a shared interest in the art of living rooted in the terroir, and intended to meet the infinite need for fresh ideas. In the hamlet, a "beauty farm" offers a high-altitude spa based on the five elements associated with the site: stone from the glaciers, wood, running water, fire, and earth. This was a natural extension of the owners' concern for the well-being of their guests, who already had the benefit of a sauna, an outdoor Swedish bath, an indoor swimming pool, and a line of beauty and health-care products based on mountain plants.

It all started with a collection of furniture and Savoy chalets, and a tremendous intuitive feeling that the soul of a heritage could be stirred: not a heritage to be admired in a museum, but to be experienced in an enchanting setting where the guest feels at

LEFT

The decoration at Les
Fermes de Marie is
characterized by the
authenticity of the mate-
rials and the charm of
the details, but the style
is slowly evolving and
developing ever-cleaner
lines.

home while at the same time enjoying hotel amenities. On five acres (two hectares) in a wonderful location very close to the center of Megève, the seventy-one rooms, including eight suites, are divided between nine chalets, which are several hundred years old. The patina of age throughout the hamlet, and the attention paid to the authenticity of every last door handle, make this a place from a different era. The couple uses the services of a whole network of craftsmen who have the perfect skills to meet their expectations. They are great lovers of old wood, but when necessary they prefer to use new wood rather than cheat with wood that is artificially aged. For the interior, Jocelyne never wearies of old local furniture, which is "friendly and always so pretty," and she still gets carried away by "a Maurienne pole chest or a carved closet from the Bessans valley, in a naive, unsophisticated style." Her decoration is a skilful blend, and she takes care to let every room in the chalet breathe. With its exposed beams, large wood fireplaces, and rough stone walls, the architecture of the place also benefits from innumerable details scattered in just the right places to give this chalet its refined mountain character: a frieze to ornament a room number, a carved Savoyard motif, a flowered fabric, a lamp base, and so on.

Since Les Fermes de Marie opened in 1989, its style and atmosphere have greatly inspired both private individuals and hoteliers, but it would take more than that to make Jocelyne complacent: "Our concept has not changed, but the interior decoration is continually updated from season to season. We are very far from the caricature we started out with: salt glaze pottery, dried flowers, and lava tiles. . . . The mountain character is still very clear, but the style is now much cleaner." ❄

Running water is as essential here as wood; in addition to the swimming pool, Swedish bath, and sauna, Les Fermes offers its guests a spa reserved for beauty and health treatments.

Hauteluce et Chatel

In the hamlet of Les Choseaux on the plateau of the Arbois mountains, two farms have been completely restored and can be rented by the week or month. This is the ideal place, winter or summer, to escape with family or friends. In these mazes of old wood, a sense of harmony has been worked into every last detail, and nothing can disturb visitors' tranquility as they enjoy a life centered around the rustic, pyramid-shaped fireplace. The sensuousness of the materials used—untreated or patinated wood, terracotta floor tiles, old pottery, soft, warm fabrics—helps to create a happy atmosphere. Let us not forget that, in these reinvented farms, life is no longer about hard work. Instead of a stable and cheese dairy, one of them now has an indoor swimming pool and a sauna. And if we are worn out by leisure activities like skiing, good food and massage are among the services offered.

Jean-Louis Sibuet took down three or four high-mountain pasture chalets to create the two we see here. He had to sort through every piece in order to keep only those in good condition, whether they could be used later as they were, or would need to be reworked. He then reassembled them to carry out his project: to build into the slope two large Savoyard chalets that looked as if they had always been there, with the sort

In an isolated spot facing
the Aravis range, these
two large chalets are
ideal for lively vacations.

Under the scalloped
balustrade of the mez-
zanine, the impression
of vastness is offset by
the inclusion of recesses
here and there, creating
a feeling of privacy.

LEFT

The light pouring in is a delightful surprise in this chalet, where comfort and good cheer are the keynotes.

RIGHT

The staircase and mezzanine structure the space in the large living room, where guests can get together after skiing to enjoy a glass of mulled wine around the fire.

of view, space, and level of comfort that would attract the most demanding of customers both in France and from abroad. With their stone bases surmounted by wood, large balconies, and small-paned windows, they blend in with the landscape in the purest mountain tradition. Who would guess from the outside that these twin chalets are connected at basement level so that large families or professional sports teams can get together here in groups of more than twenty? They also function separately; the chalets do not overlook one another, and there is a stretch of grass between them, which ensures privacy for guests who have come to the country for a refreshing break, be they captains of industry, international film stars, or just ordinary people. Light reflects off the old wood panels and patinated antique furniture (picked up locally and restored) and gives a particular brightness to these spacious rooms, with their many little windows. In the winter, at about five in the afternoon, when the sun is disappearing behind the Aravis range, the houses are filled with the magical glow of the sunset. In one of the chalets it comes in through the window in the attic bedroom, envelops it in a warm atmosphere, flows down a corridor bordered by large dressing rooms, and ends up shining onto the corner bath on the opposite side of the chalet. At the same time of day in the other chalet, everyone gets up from the bench seats facing the huge open fire and moves over to the smaller, more intimate living room in order to gaze directly out at this most spectacular daily event. ☀

ABOVE AND RIGHT

The owners changed their lives in order to entertain guests as one would entertain friends. Decoration and communication became their jobs.

No one should judge the place by the austere portrait of the grandfather; everything here is designed to appeal to both children and grown-ups.

Le Chalet d'Adrien
(Adrien's Chalet)

{VERBIER, SWITZERLAND}

Adrien Turkheim fell in love with this place and wrote about it in 1903, in an account of his journey over the canton of Valais. His granddaughter Brigitte followed in his footsteps, and eventually moved here with her husband, Eric Cachart, to run a guesthouse in a large chalet where—in her dream— everyone would feel as if they were at home. Located above Verbier at the foot of the ski slopes, Adrien's Chalet faces one of the most beautiful vistas in Verbier, over the Grand-Combin massif, Mont Vélan, and the Alpine range. Constructed on the foundation of an old hotel by the architect J.-F. Michelod, it has twenty-five rooms named after flowers, to give it the warm ambience that makes it so successful. Old wood plays an essential role here. The floor is in Burgundy stone, and some of the walls are covered in waxed plaster. The rest of the decoration is the result of a subtle balance in the choice of objects such as old Russian furniture, a Poitou fireplace, and the grandfather's herbarium. Within this gentle atmosphere, there is an unobtrusive sense of luxury, with large terraces facing due south, a spa, a swimming pool (half of which is indoors), a children's playroom, and an expert chef. ☀

Le Pré Rosset
(The Rosset Meadow)

{MEGÈVE, FRANCE}

Well away from the avalanche corridors, this is a real high-mountain pasture chalet, which gets an exceptional amount of sunshine and is a wonderful place to rediscover the silence of the peaks. The façade is covered in *tavaillons,* and the small windows let in only a small amount of light. From the meadow there is a magical view over the cirque of the Véry Pass, Mont Charvin, and the Aravis range. The real luxury of the place lies in the landscape and the return to simplicity. There is the transparency of the air, and the gentle music of the water running continuously into the *bachal,* a roughly hollowed-out tree trunk that serves as a drinking trough. But there are also delicious aromas to whet the appetites of the visitors: suckling pig roasted over the fire, nettle soup, Tarentaise *crozets* (a local type of pasta), and rhubarb or blueberry tarts. Guests eat at an old table made in the area, sitting on wooden chests right next to the huge stone fireplace, over which a pork stew may well be simmering.

Paradoxically, wood and fire both reign supreme here. They create a warm atmosphere, much more intimate under these low ceilings than in resort or village chalets, where cathedral-like spaces are the norm. In the high-mountain pasture, wood

ABOVE

Before the craze for skiing brought the word "chalet" into general use, it specifically referred to this type of home in the high-mountain pasture.

LEFT

Jocelyne's paintings and Jean-Louis's woodcarvings blend with antiques they have unearthed to create a sense of gentle nostalgia.

fittings and furniture are plain and simple. The box bed by the window with its scalloped edges is unusually elaborate for this high altitude, and the freestanding dresser, with its Savoyard pottery, although simply made, is almost an extravagance. All it really takes is a tin milk jug, a shelf with a lace runner, and an earthenware coffee pot to arouse a sweet feeling of nostalgia, which will either overwhelm us or reconcile us with the passing of time.

Only a privileged few have the right credentials to come here and savor dishes as authentic as the décor. Clients of the Compagnie des Hôtels de Montagne have exclusive access to this high-mountain pasture restaurant, which was a clever idea dreamed up by Jocelyne and Jean-Louis Sibuet as a way of symbolically reliving traditional summer migration, and experiencing all the sense of freedom and luminosity that it brings. Those who wish to prolong the charm of silence until dawn can stay over. They have a choice between four little bedrooms, which would have to be described as almost monastic, if not for the fresh touch of classic red gingham curtains. At dawn, once the single shutter has been pushed open, there are fields of gentian stretching out as far as the eye can see. After that, guests who have sharp powers of observation may well spot a marmot, a chamois, or—who knows?—perhaps a capercaillie. ❋

Eden in the Alpine Garden

From Edelweiss to Bear's Ear

The mountains are a vast garden in their own right, into which a chalet made of stone and wood taken from the local environment blends unobtrusively. To plant the same sort of garden next to it as those found down on the plains would be an insult to the natural richness of the flora here. And in any case, many native plants, such as edelweiss, Venus' slipper, saxifrage, little carnation, and alpine aster, are easier to domesticate than one might imagine.

Those who try to create a classic garden will find it impossible; they will always come up against the problem of the slope, and will find themselves doing forced labor. The earth needs to be raised to form beds, then supported by little dry stone walls to prevent it from sliding downhill when battered by rain. Thus, we find tiered plots with terraces linked by picturesque flights of steps, each forming a different world: the parish priest's garden with its aromatic and medicinal herbs, the little kitchen garden, the rockery, the orchard, and so on.

In times gone by, it was the women who looked after the kitchen garden next to the chalet. In addition to herbs, it often contained flowers, berries, and fruit trees. At the Ballenberg open-air museum in Switzerland, research has been done to discover the names of the species that were cultivated in the past. Some are grown there and displayed to the public, while others seem to have been lost forever.

Today, the architecture of the garden can take the most fantastical forms, but it is always essential to begin by organizing the space. It is not just a matter of retaining the soil, but also of being "in keeping with the lines of the mountain and the harmony of the site," as nurseryman Christian Gruszka firmly believes. He recommends that conifers should not be misused to make the most of the seasons, which are so clearly defined in the mountains—not even to create hedges, a practice that does not fit in with the mountain tradition of an open landscape. If the aim is to enclose the property, one can always take inspiration from the bucolic little fences of interlaced hazel or chestnut, which used to protect the kitchen garden from cattle and wild game. Gruszka suggests, for example, that private individuals can create a garden, supported by a stone wall, that brings together all sorts of alpine elements: a petrifactive spring, a little brook, and a pond next to a peat bog. All around is a bank of crystalline rocks and another of limestone, representing a scree zone, but also an area of *lapiaz,* which are rocks with distorted shapes created by erosion.

UV-Resistant

With such clearly defined seasons, it would be wrong to think only of the danger of frost. The most important thing that all plants at high altitude have in common is the need to resist the sunlight, which is incredibly rich in ultraviolet rays. If they often appear stunted above the alpine level—in other words, on average at 11,500 feet (3,500 meters) on south-facing slopes and at 8,500 feet (2,600 meters) on north-facing ones—it is because they increase their chances of survival by reducing their exposed surface. Christian Gruszka even goes so far as to describe the arolla pine, mugho pine, creeping willow, juniper, and service tree as "true living monuments," given the evidence of their distorted forms. There are some plants that, in order to survive, cover themselves in waxy matter or hair, or make themselves particularly tough. They also need to stand up to the winter, ideally under a blanket of snow, which insulates them from the cold by maintaining a comfortable temperature of around 32°F (0°C). That is why it is not surprising that the same annual planted at the same time in the valley and at high altitude can turn out to be so disappointing in the mountains. For plants to be resistant, it is better to buy them from local nurseries, where they are raised gently in realistic conditions, and have time to build up good root defenses.

But even these adapted species are not desert plants; although there is an abundance of water in the mountains from glaciers and streams, they all need to be watered regularly, including rockery plants. This means that, despite the great capacity of flora for drawing up water from deep underground, they should not be plated in overly arid soil.

What goes into the garden depends on the altitude. At everlasting snow level, glacier wormwood and some other species can be planted successfully. Lower down at the alpine level, where the high-mountain pasture and the highest ski resorts are located, it is easier to create a garden worthy of the name using alpine varieties and hardy perennials selected by researchers for their resistance up to 11,500 feet (3,500 meters)—7,200 to 11,500 feet (2,200 to 3,500 meters) on south-facing slopes, 5,600 to 8,200 feet (1,700 to 2,500 meters) on north-facing ones. It is essential to take into consideration the recommended sun exposure and soil conditions if planting is to succeed.

Plants worth mentioning just for the pleasure of visualizing them are the alpine clematises, various types of broom, edelweiss, arnica, wormwood, mountain cumin, alpine forget-me-not, valerian, epilobium or willow-herb, houseleek, veronica, and Caucasian pincushion flower. Some of them would be worth having for their names alone, if they did not have other assets as well, notably their colors: bear's ear, Shetland mouse-ear, lion's foot, devil's bit, common evening primrose, and goldenrod, to name but a few. Many of them have their own particular appeal: poet's narcissus is fragrant, sweet cicely has splendid blooms, arquebus smells of liqueur, erodium looks like geranium, and columbine resembles a long-beak crane.

The idea of links between plants is common—for instance, between blue alpine thistle, *Achillea ptarmica* (sneezewort), dwarf rhododendron, lady's mantle, musky chervil, burnet, and day lilies. Equally irresistible are campanulas and gentians, Canadian hydrangeas, amelanchiers, and dogwood, not to

mention calamints, clusterheads, gray-leaf crane's bills, mulleins, marjoram, some of the lychnis, and borage, which is adulated in Asian countries for its whiteness. Rock ferns and some grasses can also thrive here. Produce from the kitchen garden includes rhubarb, raspberries, gooseberries, medlars, and, of course, blueberries. Oddly enough, some alliums, such as chives, are particularly exuberant at high altitude, as is wild thyme, while gypsophila grows wonderfully in the gaps in walls. Climbing shrubs that do especially well here are the alpine rose bush, with its pink flowers, highly decorative rosehips, and very beautiful foliage, and the burnet rose, which has yellow flowers and black rosehips. Those who are interested in the mountain flora beyond the limits of their own square patch can visit the extraordinary botanical garden at Lautaret, which was created before the first French ski resorts appeared, and is at 6,750 feet (2,000 meters), on the way into the Ecrins National Park in the Upper Alps. There is also the alpine garden at the Musée National d'Histoire Naturelle (National Museum of Natural History) in the Jardin des Plantes in Paris, where visitors will find some delightful surprises. Farther down, at the level of the "montagnettes" and reaping meadows (4,900 to 7,200 feet [1,500 to 2,200 meters], depending on whether the slope is south- or north-facing), the choice of planting increases as the growing conditions become less harsh. Farther down still, at the mountain village level, we find sycamore maples, hazel trees, cembra pines, larches, and birches flourishing in their turn. More than anywhere else, the mountain soil is full of stones that endlessly reappear, sometimes making us feel that our efforts to remove them and heap them into piles at the end of the flowerbed are in vain. But perhaps those piles are like cairns, symbols to the passing mountain walker of the hopes and joys that inspire the nature lover. As well as energy expended, there is energy replenished through the search for harmony in an environment of infinite resources. ✳

BIBLIOGRAPHY

Architecture, Interior Design, Crafts

ARMAND, HÉLÈNE, and JEAN-MARC BLACHE. *Chalets.*
Grenoble: Didier Richard, 1999.

BRUSSON, JEAN-PAUL. *Architecture et qualité des lieux en montagne.*
Grenoble: Collection Ascendances, H.S., 1998.

DUBOST, FRANÇOISE, editor. *L'Autre maison.*
Paris: Autrement, 1998.

MILLER, JUDITH, and JAMES MERRELL. *Maisons en bois.*
Paris: Flammarion, 1998.

PERETZ, JEAN-CLAUDE. *Art populaire: richesse des pauvres.*
Rodez, France: Éditions du Rouergue, 2001.

PERRIAND, CHARLOTTE. *Une vie de création.*
Paris: Odile Jacob, 1998.

PUIBOUBE, DANIEL. *Restaurer une maison régionale en France.*
Paris: Rustica, 1994.

SAHAROFF, PHILIPPE, and AGNÈS DE WARENGHIEN. *Chalets de montagne.* Paris: Éditions du Chêne, 1996.

———, PHUONG PFEUFER *(vol. 1),* and MARIE-CATHERINE CHAUVEAU *(vol. 2). Le style chalet.*
Paris: Rustica, 1999 and 2005.

STEIN, ANNICK. *Les Maisons de montagne.* Paris: Eyrolles, 2001.

STRUTHERS, JANE. *Splendeur du bois.* Paris: Flammarion, 1992.

VÉRY, FRANÇOISE, and PIERRE SADY. *Henry Jacques Le Même : architecte à Megève.* Liège, Belgium: Mardaga, 1988.

WEDEKIND, BEATE. *Intérieurs de montagne.*
Cologne: Taschen, 2003.

Supplementary reference: *Archiscopie.* Paris: Cité de l'architecture et du patrimoine.

Tourism

COUSIN, SYLVIANE, CLAUDE ROYER, and FRANÇOIS SIGAUT.
Le Guide du patrimoine rural. Paris: La Manufacture, 1991.

DOMPNIER, MARTHE and PIERRE. *Le Guide de la Maurienne.*
Paris: La Manufacture, 1991.

GRADOS, JEAN-JACQUES. *Le Guide du Queyras.* Paris:
La Manufacture, 1987.

GSCHWEND, MAX, PAUL FEHLMANN, and RUDOLF
HUNZIKER. *Ballenberg, Das Schweizerische Freilichtmuseum.*
Aarau, Switzerland: AT Verlag, 1982.

MOHR, JEAN, and LOUIS GAULIS. *La Suisse insolite.*
Vevey, Switzerland: Mondo, 1971.

ZARKA, CHRISTIAN. *Savoie: hommes et paysages.*
Paris: Collection Terroirs, Éditions du Chêne, 1990.

ZEGIERMAN, FRÉDÉRIC. *Le Guide des pays de France du Sud.*
Paris: Fayard, 1999.

Botany

ROMAIN, JACQUELINE, and PATRICK FOCQUET. *Fleurs de Provence et des Alpes du Sud.* Nice, France: Serre, 1997.

Supplementary reference: *Les Plantes médicinales des Alpes.*
Paris: Delta, 2000.

Les Plantes vivaces. Paris: Société Nationale d'Horticulture de France, 1989.

Litterature, Essays

MOHR, JEAN, and JOHN BERGER. *Une autre façon de raconter.*
Paris: Maspero, 1982.

ROUSSEAU, JEAN-JACQUES. *La Nouvelle Héloïse [1761].*
Paris: La Pléiade, Gallimard.

———, *Les Confessions [1771].* Paris: La Pléiade, Gallimard.

Restoration Consultants

MAISONS PAYSANNES DE FRANCE
(Government-approved landmark protection assoc.)
8, passage des Deux-Sœurs, 75009 Paris, France
Tel. +33.1.44.83.63.63
www.maisons-paysannes.org
Représentants départementaux bénévoles
(State Delegate Volunteers) Tel. by department:
Alpes-de-Haute-Provence: +33.4.92.62.53.33
Hautes-Alpes: +33.1.47.70.38.44
Isère: +33.4.76.08.03.17; +33.4.74.90.20.34;
and +33.4.74.27.15.65
Savoy: +33.4.79.28.53.22

COMPAGNONS DU DEVOIR
10, rue Mabillon, 75006 Paris, France
Tel. +33.1.44.78.22.50
www.compagnons.org

VIEILLES MAISONS FRANÇAISES
93, rue de l'Université , 75007 Paris, France
Tel. +33.1.40.62.61.71
www.vmf.net

C.A.U.E. (Conseil d'Architecture, d'Urbanisme et de
l'Environnement) Tel. by department:
Annecy: +33.4.50.33.50.03
Gap: +33.4.92.51.73.58
www.fncaue.asso.fr

Tourism

MAISON DE SAVOIE
31, avenue de l'Opéra, 75001 Paris, France
Paris: +33.1.42.61.74.73
Tel. by department:
Chambéry: +33.4.79.85.2.45 (Savoy)
Annecy: +33.4.50.51.32.31 (Haute-Savoie)

SWITZERLAND TOURISM
Head Office
Tödistrasse 7, 8027 Zurich, Switzerland
Tel. +41.1.288.11.11
www.myswitzerland.com

You can contact these organizations and other tourism offices
to receive information, maps, and guides that will give you
ideas for visits to local sites (gardens, museums, villages,
traditional dwellings, and so on). Eventually you can develop
an Alpine flavor in your interior decoration style and become
an expert at antiquing...

Crafts, Interior Design, and Antiques

ANTIQUITÉS CATHERINE TISSOT-NAVARRO
2142 route du Praz-sur-Arly, 74120 Megève, France
Tel. +33.4.50.58.98.38
www.decoration-navarro.com

ANTIQUITÉS VEYRET
Route d'Annecy, 74230 Thônes, France
Tel. +33.4.50.02.15.56

BOIVIN (moldings and balconies)
35, rue Jean Morin, 74800 La Roche-sur-Foron, France
Tel. +33.4.50.25.94.31

LES BROCANTAIRES
3401, route Nationale, 74120 Megève, France
Tel. +33.4.50.21.42.10

LIBRAIRIE DES ALPES
6, rue de Seine, 75006 Paris, France
Tel. +33.1.43.26.90.11
www.librairie-des-alpes.com

POTERIE DE MARNAZ
Rue de la Poterie, 74460 Marnaz, France
Tel. +33.4.50.98.35.49

POTERIE HERMANN
La Côte, 74570 Evires, France
Tel. +33.4.50.62.01.90

SECCOTINE
Résidence Squaz Valley 2, 73150 Val-d'Isère, France
Tel. +33.4.79.41.90.23

Nursery

CHRISTIAN GRUSKA
76, chemin Foray, 73160 Cognin, France
Tel. +33.4.79.68.75.51

Architects and Interior Decorators

BERNARD ROSIER
25, allée de la Belle au Bois, 74120 Megève, France
Tel. +33.4.50.21.27.19

GUY THODOROFF (Le Zodiac)
Avenue de la Gare, 3962 Montana, Switzerland
Tel. +41.27.481.19.45
sart@bluewin.ch

CONCEPT JOCELYNE ET JEAN-LOUIS SIBUET
(Compagnie des Hôtels de Montagne)
Chemin de Riante Colline, 74120 Megève, France
Tel. +33.4.50.93.03.10
www.c-h-m.com

ALAIN PERRIER (Générale d'Agencement)
87, rue de Chambéry, BP 20, 73230 St Alban-Leysse, France
Tel. +33.4.79.33.85.60
www.generale-agencement.com

ARTHEMA
18, allée Lac de Garde, House Boat n°6, BP 217,
73374 Le-Bourget-du-Lac, France
Tel. +33.4.79.26.23.20

CABINET JACQUES LABRO
Hameau Nicolo, 13, rue Nicolo, 75115 Paris, France
Tel. +33.1.42.88.03.67

CHRISTIAN MARTIN (ADC Architectes)
2, avenue Jeanne, 92600 Asnières, France
Tel. +33.1.47.90.78.08

Mountain House Developers

AXE & D
Parc du Calvi, RN 508, 74330 Poisy, France
Tel. +33.4.50.22.68.00
www.axe-d.com

MICHEL COVAREL (Covarel Immobilier)
19, avenue du Mont-Saint-Michel, 73000 Barberaz, France
Tel. +33.4.79.60.55.00

PATRICK SANYAS (Immobilier de prestige)
181, chemin des épis, 74120 Megève, France
Tel. +33.4.50.21.13.81

Luxury Chalet Rentals

AVORIAZ.COM. *www.avoriaz.com*
(suggestion: Chalet Arketa)

COLLINEIGE (Contact: Colleen Olianti)
239, chemin de la tannerie, 74400 Les Tines Chamonix, France
Tel. +33.4.50.53.01.88
www.collineige.com
(suggestions: Chalets Le Mazot des Tines and Guelpa)

VAL D'ISÈRE CHALETS
8-9 Marvic House, Bishops Road, London SW6 7AF, England
Tel. +44.20.3080.0222
www.valdiserechalets.co.uk
(suggestion: Chalet Les Carats)

COMPAGNIE DES HÔTELS DE MONTAGNE
(see above)
(suggestions: Chalets Hauteluce and Chatel)

COVAREL IMMOBILIER
(see above)
(suggestion: Chalet Anchorage)

LE CHALET D'ADRIEN
Chemin des Creux, 1936 Verbier, Switzerland
Tel. +41.27.771.62.00
www.chalet-adrien.com

LES FERMES DE MARIE
163, chemin de la riante colline, 74120 Megève, France
Tel. +33.4.50.93.03.10
www.fermesdemarie.com

PALACE HOTEL GSTAAD
Palacestrasse, 3780 Gstaad, Switzerland
Tel. +41.33.748.50.00
www.palace.ch

Hotels and Restaurants

CHESA GRISHUNA
Bahnhofstrasse 12, 7250 Klosters, Switzerland
Tel. +41.81.422.22.22
www.chesagrischuna.ch

HÔTEL LE MÉLÉZIN
Rue de Bellecôte, 73120 Courchevel, France
Tel. +33.4.79.08.01.33

HÔTEL LE MONT BLANC
Place de l'Église, 74120 Megève, France
Tel. +33.4.50.21.20.02
www.hotelmontblanc.com

LA FRUITIÈRE
Chalet Abate, BP 26, 73150 Val-d'Isère, France
Tel. +33.4.79.06.01.47
www.lafoliedouce.com

Acknowledgments

Philippe Saharoff would like to thank each owner for their kind welcome during the making of this book, and especially:
Peggy Brozeck, Colleen Olianti, Jocelyne Sibuet, Alain Perrier, Jean-Michel Villot, and Luc Reversade.

Published in 2007 by Stewart, Tabori & Chang
An imprint of Harry N. Abrams, Inc.

Library of Congress Cataloging-in-Publication Data

Leprat, Gwenaëlle.
  [Vivre à la montagne. English]
  Mountain houses / photographs by Philippe Saharoff ; text by Gwenaëlle Leprat.
    p. cm.
  Originally published: Vivre à la montagne. Paris : Aubanel, 2005.
  Includes bibliographical references and index.
  ISBN 10: 1-58479-648-0 (alk. paper)
  ISBN 13: 978-1-58479-648-0 (alk. paper)
  1. Architecture, Domestic—France—Alps, French. 2. Architecture, Domestic—Switzerland—Alps, Swiss.
  3. Hillside architecture—France—Alps, French. 4. Hillside architecture—Switzerland—Alps, Swiss.
  5. Interior decoration—France—Alps, French. 6. Interior decoration—Switzerland—Alps, Swiss.
  I. Saharoff, Philippe. II. Title.

  NA7590.L4713 2007
  728.0944'58--dc22
                          2007020091

Design by Séverine Morizet

Project Manager, English-language edition: Magali Veillon
Editor, English-language edition: Aiah Wieder
Designer, English-language edition: Shawn Dahl
Jacket design, English-language edition: E.Y. Lee
Production Manager, English-language edition: Tina Cameron

The text of this book was composed in Akzidenz-Grotesk BQ, ATSackers Gothic, and Perpetua.

Printed and bound in France
10 9 8 7 6 5 4 3 2

HNA
harry n. abrams, inc.
a subsidiary of La Martinière Groupe
115 West 18th Street
New York, NY 10011
www.hnabooks.com